Using Television and Video to Support Learning

A Handbook for Teachers in Special and Mainstream Schools

Edited by Steven Fawkes, Su Hurrell and Nick Peacey
with
Julie Cogill, Nicola Grove and Carol Ouvry

David Fulton Publishers
London

David Fulton Publishers Ltd
Ormond House, 26–27 Boswell Street, London WC1N 3JD

First published in Great Britain by David Fulton Publishers 1999

Note: The right of Steven Fawkes, Su Hurrell, Nick Peacey,
Julie Cogill, Nicola Grove and Carol Ouvry to be identified
as the editors of this work has been asserted by them in accordance
with the Copyright, Designs and Patents Act 1988.

Copyright © David Fulton Publishers 1999

British Library Cataloguing in Publication Data
A catalogue record for this book is available from the British Library

ISBN 1–85346–597–6

Typeset by Textype Typesetters, Cambridge
Printed in Great Britain by Bell & Bain Ltd, Glasgow

Contents

Preface

Steven Fawkes

This book is composed of papers and case studies inspired by a collaborative project begun in 1993. The project partners include SENJIT, BBC (Education), Channel 4 and NCET (now BECTa) who jointly initiated a programme of research into the actual use and potential usefulness of television resources in the classrooms of learners with Severe Learning Difficulties.

The initial research, of which elements are included in this book, informed subsequent developments not only in the provision of television resources and accompanying materials, but also in the personal and professional exchange of experiences and aspirations between teachers and advisory colleagues from around the UK. Entitled *Access to Learning*, conferences were organised in order to share inspiration and practical advice, and teachers have pursued (and continue to pursue) their own developmental activities in the context of their own schools.

It is in the spirit of these events that this book has subsequently been developed, with the intention of providing an update on teachers' experiences and findings concerning the very particular contribution that television (and increasingly multimedia resources) has to make to people's learning. The core of this book consists not of theory, but of the real practice of teachers and others working in the field who speak from experience.

The papers within this book consist of:

- extracts from research reports;
- papers from speakers at the *Access to Learning* conferences;
- reports from schools developing the themes of the conferences;
- comments on useful resources and classroom strategies;
- case studies from teachers building their own schemes;
- papers on significant issues;
- references for further reading.

Contributors

Initial research: BBC Education

Further research: Nicola Grove

Papers and articles: Julie Cogill, BBC Education; Vivian Hinchcliffe, Rectory Paddock School; Denise Sanford and David Haigh, Park School; Olga Miller, Institute of Education / RNIB; Steven Fawkes, BBC Education; Nick Peacey, SENJIT; Maureen Smith, Mental Health Media.

Follow-up research and Case Study collation: Carol Ouvry

Case study reports: Elaine Kent, Ty Gwyn School, Cardiff; Anne Krisman, Little Heath School, Romford; Angela Mallett, The Shepherd School, Nottingham; Denise Sanford, Park Special School, Wakefield; Sarah Thomas, Ickburgh School, London; Angela Wellman, Beatrice Tate School, London; and other colleagues.

As befits the collaborative nature of the project the book has an editorial board, consisting of: Steven Fawkes, Education Officer, BBC Education; Su Hurrell, Independent Educational Consultant; Nick Peacey, SENJIT, Institute of Education.

Acknowledgements

The compilers of the book wish to thank all of the contributors, including participants at the conferences, speakers, Case Study teachers and their classes, and BBC Educational Publishing for permission to reproduce some items.

Personal thanks are due to Dominique Creasey for typing.

Chapter 1

Initial research into the use of television in SLD Schools

BBC Education: Sylvia Hines and Nicola Grove

In mainstream education in 1993 research showed that television had been used extensively as a teaching and learning resource for many years, but in Special Education contexts there was less evidence. In this first chapter the research findings of the **Access to Learning** *project are explored.*

The advent of the National Curriculum required teachers to cover subjects which may be outside the direct experience of students with Severe Learning Difficulties.

As television seemed well placed to offer resource materials to assist teachers in their task of delivering such experience, a project was set up as a joint initiative between BBC Schools, Channel 4 and SENJIT (Special Educational Needs Joint Initiative for Training) to investigate over a period of years how television can best be used in the broad education of students with severe learning difficulties.

Some aims of the research were:

- to increase understanding of how children with severe learning difficulties can learn through television;
- to understand how schools television can contribute to the total education of the child with severe learning difficulties, in particular by increasing access to the National Curriculum;
- to create programmes and other resources based on these understandings;
- to increase awareness of how teachers can use television materials most effectively;
- to disseminate knowledge of the above;
- to establish an institutional structure to enable the continued development of work in this field.

The first step in this project in 1993 was therefore to carry out research amongst teachers on practical matters.

Access to Learning: The project

The use of television in SLD Schools

We wanted to learn all we could about teachers' use of and response to existing programming, both to confirm the need for a new initiative and to inform future production. This information came from two sections of a questionnaire: the first asked for general comments about programmes used, the second was a more detailed section completed with reference to the use of a particular programme.

The first question was: *'Have any television or video programmes been used with groups of pupils during this academic year?'* 94 per cent of respondents answered this question (127 teachers) and of these 74 per cent said that they had used television or video programmes. Although this figure was low when compared to mainstream schools, it was an encouraging figure, given that no specialist material had yet been made for a group of students with very particular needs. It suggested that teachers were looking to television as an educational resource. Table 1.1 shows that teachers either use the television frequently or barely at all.

How often would you say video or TV programmes are used with pupils, on average? (n=124)

	general learning difficulties	profound learning difficulties	total	%
More than once a week	23	13	36	29%
About once a week	36	12	48	39%
About once a month	13	3	16	13%
About once a term	4	2	6	5%
Less than once a term	12	6	18	14%

Table 1.1 Teachers use of television

Teachers were also asked which programmes they recalled having used and the curriculum areas in which they used them. Responses highlighted two interesting general factors.

1. A wide range of programmes was used. Very few programmes were used by significant numbers of teachers, confirming that teachers felt they need to hunt for suitable material. However, the fact that they were prepared to do so, and that they were using many programmes across curriculum areas suggested that they valued television as an education resource. The following series were mentioned most frequently in 1993: 'You and Me'; 'Words and Pictures'; 'Storytime'; 'Thinkabout Science'; 'Watch'.

2. Programmes were being used across curriculum areas. Many programmes were listed as being used in several, sometimes most, subject areas.

Attention

The comment made most frequently was that television helped improve children's concentration, so long as the programme was no more than 10–15 minutes long. This was felt equally by teachers working mainly with children with PMLD.

> 'TV programmes increase the attention span, encourage language and are good as a source of further topic work.'
> 'Can encourage real concentration and response from children with PMLD.'
> 'One school introduced a 15–30 minute session once a week to work on attention, concentration and behaviour control. Initially, three out of thirteen pupils could watch a 15 minute programme. Over a year, the ratio improved to eleven out of thirteen able to watch for up to half an hour.'

Enjoyment

This was the next most frequent comment, with teachers adding that TV could be used as a reward or motivator: 'Many pupils are most motivated by non-schools broadcasting, such as advertisements.'

Educational benefits

Television was seen as a genuine experiential backup providing positive reinforcement for learning and a major tool to promote discussion.

> 'When the appropriate level stimulates interest this can then be extended. For example, the Anglo-Saxon village in "Zig Zag" roused enough interest to warrant arranging a visit which resulted in a full project.'
> 'Television opens horizons considerably. It is good for both preparation and follow-up work.'
> 'With soap operas children will react and relate to various family dramas which are part of the plot; this helps them to discover, explore and develop an understanding of their own emotions and feelings.'
> 'Animation and movement are effective.'
> 'Helps develop listening skills.'

Teachers were asked which support materials they had found the most useful with any programme. They mentioned the following as useful support for their work:

- Teachers' materials which can be adapted. Particularly mentioned were 'You and Me', 'Zig Zag', 'Rosie and Jim', 'Words and Pictures', 'Look and Read', 'Thinkabout', 'Landmarks', 'Watch'.

- Story books accompanying programmes.
- Simple activity support sheets/worksheets (with symbols rather than words).
- Photocopiable material to reinforce programme content.
- Posters and pictures.
- Short programme notes.
- Planning sheets.

However, the ingenuity of the individual teacher was also stressed: 'We make our own!'

Particular recommendations

Several teachers mentioned the beneficial contribution of signing support, e.g. using Makaton, and the Makaton nursery rhyme video, funded by Children in Need, was extremely popular.

Teachers also highlighted the problem of excessive speech, and make specific comments about the benefits of music. 'Too much talking, and the concentration goes.'

Practical use of video equipment

An interesting feature was that many schools used a video camera extensively as a way of recording the students' activities and a couple of the comments related particularly to this:

'Self-esteem is boosted when pupils see themselves on video.'
'Making videos of outings is very much enjoyed by SLD pupils.'

The educational value of a television programme is enhanced by its context and the way in which it is used. Previous research had suggested that this was particularly true for students with learning difficulties. We therefore wanted to get a sense of exactly how the programmes were being shown, by asking the question: 'How did you use the programme?' (See Table 1.2)

When viewing, teachers' stressed points were:

'Use the pause button to illustrate points in greater depth.'
'Videos are particularly useful as they can be replayed to make a point.'

There was a range of follow-up activity:

'The class was inspired by the music to have several sessions on instruments.'
'I encouraged children to make drawings related to animals/people in response to paused video images.'
'We dramatised the story afterwards.' 'It gave an introduction to a day trip to the beach.'

How did you use the programme?

	SLD		PMLD		total
Watched the programme at the time it was broadcast	21	26%	8	42%	29%
Used a videorecording	73	90%	14	74%	89%
Previewed the programme	49	60%	9	47%	58%
Discussed the programme with the group, prior to viewing	35	43%	7	37%	42%
Watched the whole programme straight through	63	78%	16	84%	79%
Selected extracts from the programme	20	25%	1	5%	21%
Used the pause button to stop the action and comment	47	58%	10	53%	57%
Played the clip without sound	3	4%	0	0	3%
Provided your own commentary	36	44%	11	58%	47%
Watched the programme more than once with the group	50	62%	11	58%	61%
Used follow-up materials provided for the programme	24	30%	4	21%	28%
Made own materials	63	78%	16	84%	79%

Table 1.2 The number of responses is followed by the percentage of the sample this represented

Perceived problems with using television

Teachers felt that existing mainstream material was often inappropriate and difficult to use with these students, the greatest problems being the level of complexity of the programmes and the amount of information that they contained. 'For younger children the facilities are great, but there is a need for age-appropriate ones for teenagers.'

A further question asked what problems teachers experienced with the programmes they had used. See Table 1.3.

Curriculum priorities: Lifeskills

This was without doubt the area (together with PSHE) where people felt television could be of most value. The curriculum priorities of respondents showed that self-help skills were seen as by far the most important area.

Were there any problems in using the programme?

	SLD	PMLD	total
Yes	32	9	41
No	25	3	28
Please tick any of the following which apply:			
Programme speed (of commentary, flow of ideas)	23	8	31
Picture speed, style, flashback, cuts	11	-	11
Programme too long	7	1	8
Language too difficult	27	11	38
Too much information	22	7	29
Not enough reinforcement of concepts	27	10	37
Information/concepts too difficult	18	7	25
Information/concepts not age-appropriate	19	7	26
Lack of role models of people with disabilities	24	5	29

Table 1.3 Problems in using programmes

Age ranges	5–11	11–16	16–19
Self help	23	11	11
Sex education	4	10	20
Shopping and cooking	8	11	17
Personal hygiene	6	14	7
Personal independence	12	12	12
Relationships	9	12	12
Roads and transport	10	9	10
Domestic skills	-	10	-

'Programmes dealing with: How do I get about? How do I choose what I want to do? What should I do if approached by a stranger? How do I ask for things I want? How do I make friends? as well as practical problems like cooking and making a shopping list.'

As part of the research in 1993 teachers were given specific suggestions for programmes to be made with SLD learners in mind. The results showed that teachers would definitely or probably use:

- environmental topics;
- drama and discussion of feelings and personal relationships;
- games to stimulate problem-solving and thinking skills;
- adaptations of well-known stories.

Teachers would be unlikely to want to use:

- a magazine-style programme;
- programmes illustrating historical topics.

They made suggestions about programme style:

'Easy concepts and ideas taught in age-appropriate ways. Early learning for 11 year-olds shouldn't be babyish. Use older children and adults in the programmes.'

'Keep the programmes to 10–15 minutes.'

'Use real people and situations rather than cartoons.'

'Programmes that can be broken into segments to enable use of pause button.'

'Visually stimulating, through colour and sound.'

'Positive images of SLD children and adults, in their natural surroundings.'

'SLD covers a wide range of development so curricular focus should either clearly indicate what development level it is aimed at or cover a variety of levels.'

For more profoundly disabled students:

'Programmes with repetition particularly useful, especially repetition of songs.'

'Must reflect difficulty with attention, reception, listening; so must be basic, not more than three new ideas, and practical.'

'Age-appropriate programmes for secondary/FE students are practically non-existent.'

'Anything big, bold and brassy .'

Some strong opinions were expressed:

'Pupils with profound learning disabilities have little understanding of what is happening in the programmes. It would be very difficult to produce one of value to them.'

The learners' point of view

What do students want? is perhaps the hardest question to answer. When asked about existing programmes the students tended to be uncritically positive, even though they were experienced viewers, through watching a great deal of television at home. We therefore wanted to find some further information about what students were watching and their opinions of it. A letter was therefore sent to students' parents asking for their help in keeping a viewing diary over a period of two weeks. This was a long task to maintain, and out of a total of 126 sent out, we received 36 completed diaries (28 per cent). The results confirmed teachers' reports that students watched a great deal of television, predominantly soaps ('Neighbours') or other programmes with a strong soap element (e.g. 'The Bill'). 'The Big Breakfast Show', however, was another hit.

If there was one thing that the schools visits confirmed it was that children enjoyed talking about their favourite television programmes and that 'Neighbours' was a major feature in students' discussions amongst themselves. In some lessons episodes of 'Neighbours' were already being used for PSHE work in 1993.

Chapter 2

Use of television in Special Education contexts

Nicola Grove

In this chapter the initial research findings are developed, specific issues are raised and practical guidelines are outlined in connection with viewing a television programme.

Television is so much a part of our everyday lives that we tend to take it for granted. We don't think twice about switching it on and off, changing channels, grasping what is going on midway through a programme, and dividing our attention between the screen and reading the paper, or having a conversation. However, if we think about it, we realise that we have developed the ability to do all these things over a prolonged period of time. We have learned how to use the medium efficiently.

When television and video are used in an educational setting, with pupils who have special needs, we need to think about this process of learning. Many pupils who have severe learning difficulties will be experienced viewers who have the necessary skills to attend, respond and learn from what they watch. Indeed, they may surprise us with their knowledge of the conventions of the medium. Many pupils, however, will need support to benefit from television programmes, and it cannot be expected that simply being in front of the screen will necessarily lead to learning. Other pupils may have specific impairments which interfere with their ability to process televised information.

The guidelines in this chapter aim to provide practical suggestions that will help teachers to use television successfully with all pupils. They are based on discussions with specialist advisers, and the findings of a research project carried out by the BBC and the Mental Health Media Council into teachers' use of television in SLD schools. It must be noted, however, that we know very little about the response of pupils with complex learning needs to this medium. We are all novices, or more excitingly, pioneers, and teachers are constantly developing their practice to find out what works best for them and their highly individual pupils.

We all think we know how to use and watch a video. However, experience has shown that there are good and bad ways of using video in the classroom; and that using the video as a teaching tool involves skills that don't come automatically. The following are some *do's* and *don'ts* that you may find helpful.

Planning

- Do integrate the programmes into your ongoing schemes of work in various areas of the curriculum. The research showed that pupils attended better to televised information when they were able to relate it immediately to other experiences in and outside the classroom.
- Do preview the programme before you use it. Be selective: decide which bits you would like to emphasise and use for discussion; which sections might interest particular pupils; and how you will introduce the programme, relate it to the current topic, and follow it up.
- Do check that all the equipment is in working order before you use it. There is nothing worse than preparing your class for viewing only to find that you cannot get a picture. Never assume that because it worked yesterday it will be OK today.
- Do make back-up copies of your videos, and take off the 'write-protect' tab to prevent re-recording. If you are using the medium a lot, it is inevitable that sooner or later a pupil will press the record button and wipe a programme. (Yes, it can happen, in a special assembly, in front of the whole school!)

Viewing

- Do make sure all pupils can see the screen. You will need to consider:

1. Other light sources. Watch in a slightly darkened room, with other sources of light behind, rather than in front of the monitor.
2. Height of screen. If necessary, raise the monitor by putting it on a table.
3. Positioning of pupils. Pupils with physical disabilities and pupils with visual impairments may need to take up special positions in relation to the screen. Make sure pupils are sitting upright, and making the best use of head control and existing vision. Discuss this beforehand with physiotherapists and the appropriate advisers. You might also ask parents and carers about the position the pupil adopts to watch the television at home.
4. Aids to vision and hearing. Make sure pupils are wearing glasses and hearing aids, if necessary.
5. Size of group. Watching the television is a social activity which can bring the whole class together. However, if the group is too big, it can be difficult for all pupils to see and participate in what is happening. You might like to use whole-class viewing the first

time for the programme, and then break up into small groups for repeat viewings. It is a good idea to establish some basic rules and traditions about viewing: e.g. sitting attentively, and comfortably; looking towards the screen in preparation for switching on.

6. Where you watch. It is easier to integrate use of the television into what you are doing if you can bring it into the classroom, rather than moving to a separate room.

7. Where you sit. The best place for the person taking the session to sit is on a small chair at the side where the controls to the video are easily accessible. A remote control is a real advantage. Other staff members should sit with pupils who need particular help in attending and responding to the programmes.

Teaching strategies

- Do introduce the programme to pupils. Prepare them for what they are going to watch by telling them briefly something about what to expect. You might like to go over some of the vocabulary of words and signs that they will need in order to take part in discussion.

- Do show programmes several times. All research into learning from television shows that children benefit from repetition. This allows them to develop prediction of what comes next, and recall of what they have seen. One approach which has been used successfully is to watch the programme through first as a whole, then to go back to the beginning and use the pause, review and fast forward buttons to watch selected chunks. The first showing can be used to make some observations about pupils' responses and viewing behaviour, using an Observation Form such as the one shown as Figure 2.1.

- Do use the pause button. This has been termed the 'Stop-Start' method. It allows you to organise the processing of information by pupils. You can stop the action at key points to talk about what is going on. However, don't do this on the first showing, as it can be disorientating unless an extract is completely self-contained. Pupils need to develop some ideas of the whole context first, before analysing it, You may like to use cues, like the signs for 'Stop' and 'Start' again, to make it clear what you are doing.

NB. On some videos, you get a distorting tracking image of black line when you freeze the image. If you keep pressing the pause button, it can be moved to the top or bottom of the picture. If it is really bad, you will need technical advice.

- Do reinforce active participation by the audience. Television is a wonderful stimulus for spontaneous language. Encourage children to respond to the presenter's questions, imitate what is going on, call out in surprise or excitement. Active engagement indicates the children are attending, which in turn promotes learning.

- Do make use of the natural cues to starting and finishing an activity that the television provides. These will be helpful for pupils who have difficulty with changing from one activity to another, or who have little sense of time. Encourage pupils to take it in turns to operate the

OBSERVATION FORM

Programme title _____ Date _____

Names of pupils	What did pupils do?	What was happening on the programme?

Figure 2.1

controls; turn beginnings and endings into rituals that frame the activity. For example, you might count down from ten before switching on.

Discussion after viewing

It is better to provide opportunities for discussion as you go through the programme a second time, rather than waiting till the end and requiring the pupils to recall everything that they have seen.

As a general rule of thumb, the best way to promote discussion is to ask open-ended questions, rather than closed questions which can only be answered with yes or no. These are the sorts of questions which stimulated pupil communication in the groups who took part in the research study outlined above:

What's happening/happened?
What would happen if …?
How would you/did they/will they …?
Tell me …
What do you think?
Why did …?

If you are looking for specific information, however, you may need to help pupils by narrowing down the question:

Tell me / Show me how the elephant ate the food.
Was the elephant big or little?

- Do respond to pupil contributions. Be prepared to follow creative ideas or questions introduced by pupils which indicate that they are making connections between their own experiences and what they have seen, even if it means deviating from your lesson plan! Be alert for any remarks which indicate misunderstandings – pupils may not interpret what they see in the way you expect.
- Do provide opportunities for pupils who communicate non-verbally to take part in discussions, through signs, use of communication boards, gestures, facial expressions and vocalisations. These pupils may need more time to contribute and some way of attracting attention, such as a buzzer or light.

Guidelines for adapting the use of television and video to the needs of pupils' specific impairments

Observation

Careful observation is the best way of finding out, not only what kind of adaptations may be necessary for pupils, but also which parts of the programme successfully gain their attention. The information can be used as the basis for planning subsequent viewing and follow-up work. A simple observation form such as the one shown as Figure 2.1, could be used to note which parts of the programme stimulate which responses in pupils. If you show the programme once through as a whole, this is a good time for scribbling down some notes. The following general guidelines may be helpful for thinking about a variety of special needs.

Visual impairments

Pupils may have low levels of visual acuity for two reasons. They may have actual impairments, such as peripheral or tunnel vision, cortical visual impairment or short sight, and/or they may be functioning at an early developmental level, which means that they have difficulty in perceiving and attaching meaning to visual cues, and are mainly responsive to space and movement. Even if pupils have quite severe visual problems, however, the moving images provided by the television have been found to act as a powerful stimulus for looking.

To compensate for impairments, you will need to consider a pupil's position in relation to the screen, and the use of specific aids such as protective visors – for example to reduce the effect of glare from the screen. Make sure a pupil's head is maintained at an angle which supports vision. Short-sighted pupils should sit nearer, and those affected by glare further away. Make sure the main light source is the television itself, and that the screen is cleaned regularly.

Pupils with low vision may need to learn to watch the screen. Use the television as an opportunity to train pupils' visual skills. You can use:

- TV-like materials in associated activities: a box-like surround, with a dark background in which brightly coloured objects or puppets appear and disappear. Allow the pupils to explore the objects before and after they look at them 'on screen'.
- Large pictures and photographs, outlined like a screen.
- Video images of familiar people and places.
- Computer activities. You can use the computer to build up visual attention skills of scanning, tracking and discriminating figure from ground. Some support materials consists of digitised images which can be accessed on the computer, and which may promote recognition and recall.

Hearing impairments

Pupils who are profoundly deaf, or who have hearing impairments, will be very dependent on information that is visual. Ensure that they are wearing their hearing aids, in working order, and that the volume level is appropriate.

If the pupils use Sign Language to communicate, or if you use it to support them, you will need to preview programmes and decide which parts need additional interpretation through sign. You can use the pause button to stop the action, sign what has been said, and then continue. Check that you know the sign vocabulary to use.

Dual / multiple sensory impairments

Pupils who have a combination of visual, hearing and physical impairments will need extensive support to respond to the television. They will need a staff member to sit with them, and provide multi-sensory cues to tell them when to look towards the screen, and to prompt responses. These include signing on the pupil's body, or moving the pupil's hands through a sign in response to the image on screen. Think of television viewing as a story-telling session that, in a younger child, would involve sitting on an adult's lap, with a picture book. If you observe the pupils closely, you may be able to select particular parts of programmes to which they show some response, that you can use subsequently in individual sessions.

Epilepsy

Pupils whose epilepsy is secondary to organic brain damage are most unlikely to be affected by the flickering of a television screen. However, if you think they are at risk, you should check to find out if they have photo-sensitive epilepsy. If they do, and it is not controlled by medication, they should not sit too near the screen, and should avoid watching in a very dark room, as strong contrasts can act as a trigger.

A set of guidelines on the use of television and computers with pupils who have primary epilepsy has been prepared by Hampshire Microtechnology Centre. Details from Neville Dalton, Hampshire Microtechnology Centre, Connaught Lane, Portsmouth PO6 4SJ.

Pupils using communication aids

Communication aids range from very simple boards with symbols or pictures to which the student points, to electronic communication aids with voice synthesisers. If pupils are to respond to the programme and participate in classroom discussion, they need to be positioned correctly, with their communication aid in front of them, placed at the appropriate angle for use before the programme starts, They also need to have the appropriate vocabulary actually on the board, or programmed into the system, not only for immediate use, but also for follow-up work. Preview programmes, decide which words will be needed, and discuss these with the speech/language therapist. In order to encourage active participation, you could programme some general phrases and verses from songs into one of the simpler aids, such as an Introtalker, or an Echo 4. These could if necessary be passed between non-verbal pupils, who can then press a key to shout out comments such as the following: 'yes', 'no', 'what's that?', 'look!'.

During class discussion, these pupils will need more time than verbal pupils if they are to contribute – they have to find the vocabulary on the board, and then touch the appropriate space. If pupils do not have an aid with a speech synthesiser, but are only pointing to a picture, make sure there is a staff member or friend watching who can 'voice-over' what they want to say, and that they have some means of indicating that they want to have a turn, or to interrupt, such as a buzzer or light.

Pupils with profound learning disabilities / limited understanding of language

All pupils may respond to certain images and sounds which have an interest for them. As when compensating for multiple impairments, you will need to provide a lot of cues, support and contextualisation. Preview programmes to decide how you can integrate selected parts of the programme into the ongoing work for these pupils. For example, if you are going to focus on spring flowers, it is useful to show the pupils the bulbs that are growing in the classroom, then immediately show the image on the television, then show the bulbs again.

Whilst pupils are watching the programmes in a larger group, observe them to see if they spontaneously make any gestures or vocalisations in response to what they see. Help them to make one or two signs to name images on the screen, and encourage them to reproduce these in discussion times. Pupils may be able to imitate an action or sound they have observed, take part in songs or games, and come up to touch an image on the screen.

Pupils can also make use of the computer to bring up digitised images from the programmes to recall and respond to key scenes.

Chapter 3

The developing use of television and video to support teaching

Carol Ouvry and Steven Fawkes

Following two Access to Learning Conferences at which teachers exchanged practical details of their use of television in school a second period of research is reported on in this chapter. By this time the first series of 'Go for it!' had been broadcast. This chapter looks at how the picture of use had changed between 1993 and 1995.

The purpose of this research was to gather information about the use of television and video in teaching and, in particular, to attempt to identify good and innovative practice which would provide material for other teachers to work with.

The information was gathered from teachers who had participated in *Access to Learning* conferences in Autumn 1994 and/or in December 1995. The great majority taught in all-age schools for pupils with severe or profound learning difficulties, although two of these schools were single phase, and a small number of teachers came from schools which were primarily for pupils with moderate learning difficulties or physical disabilities.

Summary of the results

Use of TV and video

Of the 32 schools taking part in the research, only four stated that they used little or no television for teaching purposes. Twenty-three used educational television and 15 used programmes for the general public.

Fourteen schools used educational videos and 12 used videos made for the general public.

For what purpose?

The majority of schools stated that TV and video was used for curriculum support: 16 used it for delivering subject knowledge and for developing skills; 8 used it to provide breadth of experience.

Advantages

Television can

- bring visual images into the classroom that are not normally accessible;
- focus on aspects of experience to highlight them;
- be used to reinforce and contextualise learning experiences;
- act as a basis for topic work;
- give access to knowledge and understanding not bound by print;
- illustrate the distinction between reality and fantasy in narrative.

TV is motivating and stimulating for SLD pupils and they can operate the technology. It is an experience that they share with the wider community – in itself it is a force for integration, and shared reference. Because pupils watch such a lot of television, they can bring their experiences into the classroom. Pupils already learn incidentally from TV – they can sing advertising jingles, know the plot of soaps, know something about dinosaurs and skeletons.

However, mainstream programmes make assumptions about cultural knowledge and background, including people from different regions, and non-English speaking backgrounds. There are few role models of people with disabilities, and the experiences portrayed are often unrepresentative of the environments with which pupils are familiar. It is hard to be sure what pupils are grasping from the programmes they have seen.

Nine schools used television to encourage pupils to be discriminating viewers, and three to develop personal preferences. TV and video was used in five schools to enable pupils to identify with their peer groups; 11 schools used it to promote awareness of different cultural traditions, often within PSE or RE sessions; five used it for discussion of current affairs and issues. TV and video was used for leisure purposes in 13 schools, mainly during wet playtimes, leisure clubs, or at the beginning or end of terms.

The majority of schools had CD ROM and multimedia resources. A few used named packages. Many seemed to be on the point of developing the use of these resources at the time of the research.

Subjects

TV and video were used in a large number of subjects, both in the National Curriculum and in alternative curricula. The subjects are listed below in order based on the number of times they were mentioned by the teachers:

English	18
PHSE	14
Geography	11
History	9

Science	9
Sensory curriculum	9
RE	8
Maths	7
Foreign Language	5
PE (including dance)	4
Cross curricular including topic	4
Drama	3
Environmental studies	2
Art	2
Music	2
Careers education	2

The following were mentioned by one school only:

Media studies, leisure, European awareness, self advocacy, cookery.

Which programmes/ videos are used?

A large number of programmes were mentioned, and teachers were not always able to identify whether these were recordings of TV programmes or specially made videos purchased from TV companies, educational suppliers or general outlets. Teachers themselves were, understandably, rather vague when giving information about programmes used by other teachers, or in other departments.

There was an obvious discrepancy between the number of times particular programmes were identified in this section, and the number of times in the first question about the use of educational or general programmes. For example, soaps were mentioned many times in the first question, but not specified in this section.

By far the most frequently identified programme was '*Go For It*' (14). Other educational programmes which were mentioned more than once were:

Makaton video	5
Watch	5
Number time	4
Words and Pictures	4
Storytime	3
Primary Science	3
Hello!	3
Health Education videos	3
Shakespeare	3
Schools History	2
Fourways Farm	2
Come outside	2
Cats Eyes	2

Other programmes or videos of interest, but mentioned less frequently were:

Talk, Write and Read	English Express	LRTV
Zig Zag	Stop, Look, Listen	French for Beginners
See How they Grow	Dorling Kindersley Science	Assembly Kit video.

Other videos or clips from programmes were used to support teaching and these included:

- prescribed texts (*Charlie and the Chocolate Factory, Around the World in 80 Days*);
- travel videos and programmes featuring representation of disabled people (e.g. a documentary on Eurostar used by a person with a disability);
- films or dramas recorded from TV (*Gulliver's Travels, Jungle Book, A Christmas Carol*, Pooh classics);
- news and weather forecasts;
- environmental programmes;
- and frequently soaps (used by teachers for a variety of purposes).

A number of suggestions were made for the sort of interesting content teachers were looking for, and these included:

- European awareness, to include travelling to the continent, passports. *Go For It!* in other countries.
- simplified demonstrations of sports, e.g. swimming;
- dance – linking it with history with traditional dancing etc.;
- geography, linking it with different cultures;
- post-19 without emphasis on work i.e. FE College, Day Centre, careers, leisure;
- daily life stories and drama depicting people with learning difficulties.

Use of TV or video with pupils with PMLD

Fifteen schools stated that TV or video was used with their pupils with PMLD. The majority used it for sensory stimulation (particularly visual stimulation). Some used the RNIB visual stimulation video for this.

Other specific uses with pupils with PMLD related to Individual Education Plans (IEP) e.g. to encourage a pupil to keep her head up or respond to an image; and for RoAs and annual reviews.

Only one teacher said that pupils with PMLD watched it as part of an integrated group. One school had made a sensory pack 'Underwater Experience' with a supporting video.

Making videos in school

Videos were made by staff in 22 schools and by pupils/students in 18 schools. They were made for a variety of purposes:

- as resource materials to support teaching (13);
- as records of activities and events (22);
- for recording experience and achievement (18);
- for the promotion of the school, mainly for parents and other schools (5);
- during inspection of the school (1);
- to give opportunities to develop technological skills (13).

These included operation of the camera and, in a few cases, the planning, scripting and directing of programmes, using the broadcast programmes to stimulate the pupils' creativity.

The resource materials and records of activities and events included a great diversity:

- science experiments;
- careers interviews;
- English assessments;
- presentations;
- keep fit;
- speech therapy;
- physiotherapy routines;
- animation;
- resources for topic weeks.

One school highlighted the need for NVQs to be created for the use of video.

Problems with using TV or video

Although many schools were enthusiastic in their use of TV and video in teaching, there were a number of difficulties which were frequently identified:

- Time of transmission of programmes. Programmes were rarely convenient for viewing at the time of transmission, and teachers often found it difficult to arrange to record a whole series. A block showing of a series helps with forward planning and consistent use of TV programmes. Repeat showings are also welcome in allowing people to make up any missed programmes.
- Programme information. Many teachers found the amount of information they receive in schools overwhelming, and did not have time to find out what was suitable for their teaching. It is always valuable to hear first-hand reviews of programmes relating to specific subjects or age-groups from colleagues as it helps to reduce the amount of research needed to find useful programmes.

- Presentation and suitability. Programmes intended for general schools use continue to pose problems for use with pupils who have learning difficulties. The problems include: (a) *Mismatch between the content and the presentation.* The issue of age-appropriate resources for students developing KS1/2 concepts remains important; (b) *Pacing.* Production style is often too fast, even if the concepts and presentation are at the right level; (c) *Language-level* inappropriate.

Other issues

Problems encountered by teachers included lack of resources:

- not enough TV monitors or video players;
- lack of aerial points;
- no editing facilities;
- lack of funds for video tapes;
- storage problems;
- access, security and maintenance problems;
- inappropriate hardware such as remote controls unsuitable for pupils to use.

Other factors are to do with time or management:

- more time for videoing and editing;
- curriculum time for use of material;
- improved management of resources;
- time for training and professional development.

Training

Many teachers felt this would be useful to encourage the use of TV and video, and to develop appropriate methodology. The following were identified as areas of training needed:

- Technical training in camera use and editing. These two skills were the most frequently mentioned.
- How to make good videos.
- Effective use of video and TV in teaching pupils with learning difficulties.
- Information about technology and linking of technology.
- Use of video by pupils/students.
- Making RoAs and portfolios of work.
- Professional exchange of ideas and networking.

Special projects

A number of schools were involved in projects which provide examples of innovative practice

1. **Beatrice Tate School, Anegla Wellman: A Cultural Project**
   This school has a very high proportion of Asian pupils and videos are brought in from the pupils' homes showing family events such as weddings (see Case Study 2 in Chapter 8).

2. **Frank Wise School, Sean O'Sullivan: Creative and Technical Skills Project**
   Students are involved in the whole process of making videos, planning, scripting, filming, and editing. For their Christmas production each class made their own individual film which was put together for a whole production. They would like to make videos on simplified sports in the future.

3. **Shaftesbury School, Clare Beckett: English module**
   They have developed an English module on TV which includes a survey of programmes and camera use.

4. **Cedar Hall School, Roger Pearce: Achievement Project**
   The students had incorporated video in their ASDAN Youth Award Scheme

5. **Little Heath School, Ann Krisman: RE Project**
   They have an award for the use of video for RE 'St Francis and the Natural World', (see Case Study 6, Chapter 8). Shortlisted for the Farmington Award for Christian education.

6. **Tweendykes School, Bob Osuch: European Project**
   The school has set up European links via video with partner schools in Belgium, Holland and Coventry on a cross curricular project.

7. **Ty Gwyn School, Elaine Ken: Animation Project**
   Video is used in a topic on animation based on the Watch with Mother programmes. The school plans to develop an Air and Water topic on video also. This is reported on later in Chapter 8.

8. **Ickburgh School, Sarah Thomas: Literature**
   Video used to make resource materials to support work on literature.

Conclusion

Teachers are making use of television programme resources in a variety of contexts, both within subjects in the curriculum and for more whole-school initiatives. Pupils and students are experiencing input of specialist educational and mainstream broadcasting, with which their teachers are interacting to support learning. Schools are finding innovative directions in their own use of video technology and are also developing skills with their students.

Chapter 4

Using television with pupils of a wide ability range

Steven Fawkes

This chapter takes a look at general principles for the use of television resources for contextualisation, stimulation and inspiration, and offers planning checklists.

As with all sorts of teaching resources television programmes are there to be used as and when the teacher thinks appropriate. One of their particular qualities is that they can be used to meet a number of objectives, depending on the age and character of a particular teaching group. The principles outlined here apply to classroom use of television resources with all sorts of audiences, of all ranges of ability.

My objective in presenting a programme clip could be wholly *experiential*, if the act of viewing a short clip is as much as the group could cope with, or if the group is developing skills of mental or physical concentration or of socialisation, or indeed, if a group is high functioning, but in need of broadening experience.

The television programme may be used in order to provide *real, multisensory experiences* through the combination of visual background (e.g. a real place elsewhere in the world), visual foreground (the body language, facial expression, conventions and appearance of real people on film), sound (in the form of voices, music, background noise) and sometimes graphics (an animation of a process) to support understanding.

This is particularly the case with some *cultural* details, which are very effectively illustrated by a programme resource. Aspects of the sensory curriculum are often strong within a programme filmed on location as it can provide a rich combination of sight and sound. This may be the first step in a sequence which can then be complemented by classroom activities involving physical movement, manipulation of real objects or symbolic representations, touch, smell and taste. The programme clip can then be revisited in order to support the development of memory skills.

Alternatively, the programme might be used to *encourage contributions* from the class, reactions to the places or people seen, recognition of particular visual or even language items, expression of opinions, reference to personal comparisons. This could well lead to *participative use*, in which the group imitates or replicates some of the items featured in the programme, joining in with a song, for example, or making their own version of a short presentation to video camera.

Language development objectives are available at a variety of levels, starting from receptive skills and progressing from the recognition of which person is speaking, through discernment of individual sounds, words or phrases to comprehension of gist and detail, supported by visual cues.

The next step may be into productive language skills where language is reproduced or adapted to personal needs, or where a narrative is retold, or a character's speech is recalled from the silent picture. Reinforcement for language previously acquired or presented away from the video screen can be achieved by spotting familiar images, people or objects in new or different contexts.

In order to avoid pupil passivity when viewing the television and to get the most from a resource, it is important for the teacher to consider particular planning issues:

Planning issues for the teacher in relation to a teaching resource

Why am I using it?
Which bit do I use for this purpose?
What preparation will the class need?
What interaction will there be?
What follow-up will there be?

Why am I using it?

What do I want out of it? This basic question of what I expect the learners to gain from the experience will determine the sort of activity I will ask them to carry out. Some examples: If I want them to work on sequencing events I will need to focus their minds on that and prepare sketches or photos to let them try it out afterwards. If I expect them to identify information from the clip I may need to pause the tape regularly in order to allow time for mental processing. If I want them to observe telephone skills and then apply them, I may need to show the same clip several times before moving over to the role-play situation. And of course I will try always to be aware of the unexpected response , and try to capitalise on opportunities for other sorts of learning.

Which bit do I use for this purpose?

A programme resource can offer a very rich, but densely packed, variety of stimuli, from which I need to be assertive in selecting the section I think will be most rewarding, within the time I have available. I can plan a variety of activities around one core item which may be revisited several times.

As a class becomes more confident in expressing its own views on television resources, it may be that a pupil will take on from time to time the mantle of providing a video clip which they particularly enjoy and presenting it to the class.

What preparation will the class need?

Preparation nearly always involves more than just introducing the topic to be investigated, and may involve highlighting particular things that the viewers are to look for, or particular language they will be encountering in the programme.

Frequently it will be helpful to establish the topic in relation to a collective or personal experience which the class has previously shared, or to a display set up on a theme in the classroom.

Questions which draw out personal responses can then be compared with the account on screen for contrasting points of view, for illustrating diversity or similarity, for challenging prejudice or stereotypes, or for encouraging negotiation: 'What's your favourite food?' 'What does he say his favourite is?' 'If he was here, what would you give him to eat?'

What interaction will there be?

What questions will I ask? The matter of interacting with the programmes is particularly important in order to develop concepts or encourage response. Possibilities include:

- pausing;
- viewing with no sound;
- watching in slow motion;
- replaying a clip;
- focusing on different areas of the screen;
- repeating words;
- commenting on images;
- personalising the topic;
- choosing;
- or even predicting what might happen next.

All engage the viewer in thinking more about the experience and help to make a stronger impact.

What will we do next?

Experiential, multisensory experiences
Programmes can be useful in supplying an initial context for a topic,

setting the scene and conveying an atmosphere, or alternatively can be used to revisit or consolidate a topic by illustrating it in a new context.

A television series uses the combination of colour, sound and often music in order to provide a rich experience, which can be linked with active participation in the classroom (movement, creative work, cross-curricular work). Very often a graphical feature or a musical feature can provide an exciting stimulus for display work or a drama activity, while a transactional situation can inspire problem-solving questions or roleplay.

Real objects which allow the learners to explore further or to reproduce a version of what they have seen are invaluable in reinforcing language and concepts, while a progression to using symbolic representations (photographs, colour pictures, line drawings, symbols and eventually words taken from the programme) can support the development of relevant literacy skills.

Cultural

Much cultural information about places, social sights and contexts or people's lifestyle is included in visual montages, and in the background of scenes. In order to explore them the teacher may well wish to show a clip several times, maybe using the pause button to pick out a particular detail for discussion.

Encouraging contributions

The power and range of visual images can help in getting a group to respond to certain topics or situations. The response can be at a variety of levels including:

- observation;
- comparison with the pupil's own experience;
- comparison with other images on screen or real objects and visuals in class;
- description of a scene or a process;
- offering of opinions or anecdotes;
- sequencing;
- making notes (by a range of means, such as poster-making, classifying images, organising photographs, creating multimedia, or making video comments);
- further research.

Similarly interviews and spoken presentations on screen adapt well to similar activities in the classroom within groups or as a whole class activity, while the visual force of TV programmes provides many opportunities for display or modelling.

Participative

Some specific features of programmes invite particular interaction, such as questions, songs, methods and rhymes. Musical items can encourage learners to develop their response to rhythm or their own self-expression with sounds, instruments and movement. Musical work can also be inspired by visual content or sound effects. For pupils who need an active physical experience opportunities exist for the teacher to develop other sorts of interaction by pausing the tape, rewinding, replaying more slowly or with the sound off, or hiding the picture in order to focus on sounds. Visual montages or paused scenes can provide material for a version of Kim's Game, to train the memory and recycle language learnt from the programme.

Because the television belongs to the real outside world of which learners have their own personal experience, it provides a learning stimulus which can be relevant to a very wide range. The selection of appropriate, interesting and relevant materials then becomes crucial, and, as ever, it is the teacher who is best placed to do this, with their own objectives and their own specific learners in mind.

Appendix: Twenty questions – a checklist

The sort of questions which teachers use after viewing a programme clip will depend on the particular context, of course. This list aims to provide some useful headings for thought:

Generic – questions to focus on opinions
Did you enjoy that?
What did you like best?

Generic– questions to focus on personal comparisons
Have you done / do you have anything like that?
Is your (house) like that?
What does (the house) look like?
What's the same?
What's not the same?

Viewing a method/sequence – questions to focus on content
Could you do that? e.g. Could you prepare a meal for two?
Where would you do it?
What would you *need* to (do that)? e.g. What would you need to go shopping with?
What would you *need* first?
What would you *do* first? Next? After that?
How would you (do that)? e.g. How would you get to the shop?
What should you be careful about?

Viewing a narrative – questions to focus on understanding and interpreting
Who are the people in the story?
What are they like?
Where are they?
What happened in the story?
What did X do / say (at a particular moment)?
What happened when X did / said that?
How did Z feel when that happened?
What do you think about Y?

Chapter 5

Television and multimedia: recording achievement and creating resources

Denise Sanford and David Haigh

*This chapter is based on a workshop at the **Access to Learning** Conference. Denise Sanford and David Haigh of Park School in Wakefield consider issues of recording achievement and involving students in the production of video and multimedia resources.*

Pupils throughout the school have personal video tapes of their experiences and achievements within school and outside. These augment their Record of Achievement folders. The videos are shown at Annual Reviews, and throughout the term pupils enjoy watching and remembering past events where they are the 'star players'. The more senior pupils have the opportunity to use the video camera themselves, and so have greater control over what goes on their RoA video. They also have access to a video player and TV in their common room and will frequently select personal videos to watch in their free time. All school events such as sports day, Christmas concert and residentials are videoed and may be downloaded to individual's tapes or shown on their own. This provides an opportunity for much discussion.

Pupils' own video of experiences

Interviews link with the RoA videos. Senior pupils undergo mock interviews on camera. The playback provides opportunities to discuss how they put themselves over (and frequently reveals a gap in their knowledge of personal details!). They also have the opportunity to interview each other.

Interviews

Still video images captured with a Canon Ion camera may be downloaded onto VHS tape using a video recorder. The easiest method we have found is to use a combination TV/Video (no wires to confuse!). Sound is added by plugging a microphone into the audio in socket. Pupils have a good understanding of the principles involved

Creating TV programmes using a Canon Ion camera and microphone

and are able to control the mixing of the images and the sound more easily than when using moving video.

Creation of multimedia using video, sound and still images on the computer

A new venture for us has been the production of our own multimedia resources. Using authoring software we have a careers resource which introduces the senior curriculum. The 'story' begins with a photo of the whole class at the bus station. By clicking the mouse or using the touch screen to select individual pupils the user is taken through college link courses at three different centres, work experience, independent travel and the independent use of leisure facilities in Wakefield. Video is used at each stage together with the voices of the pupils themselves explaining what they are doing. The aim has been that this software be used lower down the school to prepare pupils for the senior class.

Video recordings

Three types of video camera are used regularly in school:

- VHS;
- C format camcorder;
- Canon Ion still video camera.

Every student has a VHS video which is a compilation of short, edited recordings of their experiences during their school career. The older students are more involved with the whole process of recording and editing. The more competent are able to select a video, load it in the player and relive their favourite experiences. These videos are used in Annual Reviews and Careers Interviews and copies may be taken home.

The camcorder is used more frequently for teaching videoing skills as it is easier to handle. The senior students have time-tabled media lessons where they learn:

- use of the controls;
- framing techniques;
- lighting considerations;
- camera control whilst following a subject.

They have instant feedback through the TV and are encouraged to evaluate their work.

Canon Ion still video camera

The Canon Ion camera stores up to 50 still video images on a magnetic disc. There are no processing costs as images are viewed through the TV. Images may be erased and the disc reused.

The advantages of using the Canon Ion camera in the classroom are:

- teaching camera skills without additional expense;
- instant feedback;
- playback facilities – the ability to review and advance the film;
- remote control and 'interval' mode enable all students to review recordings;
- use of a digitiser allows selected pictures to be stored on the computer and used in future applications, e.g. DTP, word processing and presentation applications;
- ease of producing multimedia applications – selected pictures may be moved onto VHS for the students to add their own commentary or favourite music.

Useful CD-ROMs

- Stories: Broderbund's 'Living Books', Oxford's 'A Christmas Story', Dorling Kindersley's 'PB Bear's Birthday Party';
- Music: 'Sing Along with Dr T', Microsoft's 'Musical Instruments';
- Reference: Microsofts' 'Musical Instruments', Microsoft's 'Dangerous Creatures';
- Curriculum links: DK's *The Way Things Work*, DK's *My First Incredible Amazing Dictionary*.

The Americans have coined the phrase 'edutainment', and that is just what learning through CD ROM is. CD ROMs add a new dimension to teaching and learning. Pupils are better motivated and have greater control over what they learn. Many CD ROMs offer stimulus otherwise unavailable to the ordinary class teacher, e.g. hearing musical instruments from around the world.

Powerpoint presentations

Pupils in Year 9 and above have been involved in making simple presentations on the computer for use lower down in the school. The topics so far have been 'Road Safety', 'College Link Courses' and 'Wakefield – My City'. Pupils use the Canon Ion camera to take photos which are then put into the Powerpoint software in a slide show. Pupils organise the slide into an order to their liking and add voice-overs. The slide show can then be controlled by mouse clicks or the touch screen and so becomes accessible for those with little fine motor coordination.

Advantages of using multimedia with SLD students

- *Visual stimulation of the screen:* There is a theory that autistic pupils have a 2D view of the world and that the TV screen 'world' is more acceptable than real life. This may apply to some SLD students.
- *Control of input:* Video/computers allow for repetition of pictures, animation and sound effects. The predictability of the images may be important for some pupils, especially those with autistic tendencies.
- *Synthesised voice:* Some pupils respond better to a synthesised voice, devoid of human expression which conveys the social nuances some SLD pupils find so hard to comprehend.
- *Avoidance of human interaction:* This is a definite asset for those who find social interaction difficult at times. Computers may act as a bridge between their world and the world we want them to function in.

- *Opportunities for group interaction:* e.g. 'Living Books' – children sharing the story, the humour, the decision making.
- *Students in total control of learning environment:* Learners are able to move forwards, backwards, repeat, explore a new world under their own control, e.g. Sing Along with Dr T.
- *Differentiation:* A good CD ROM for SLD pupils, e.g. *Grandma And Me*, enables the student to read, play, or explore at different levels. As with Tom and Jerry cartoons, the humour appeals to all ages and so age appropriateness is not a problem with the *Living Books* CD ROMs.
- *Broadening horizons:* Multimedia allows exploration in areas apparently beyond their world but which they readily accept and use as starting points for further exploration, e.g. Dangerous Creatures, Musical Instruments.
- *Improved technical skills:* These include mouse control and ability to find their way through a program because the reward is so great and stimulating. Pupils' technical skills are developed for accessing the latest PC/TV multimedia machines in the High Street.

Update

Video recordings: the C format camcorder has now been replaced by the 8 mm camcorder. Students make good use of these in Transition Teams, investigating the world of work.

Canon Still Video Camera: There is now a vast range of digital cameras on the market including the chunky Sony Mavica camera which uses an ordinary floppy disc and is easy for pupils to use, as they see what they are photographing on an LCD screen on the camera itself. Up to 30 images are stored on the disc, which can then go straight into the computer. This camera has revolutionised our record-keeping; it goes everywhere with us and images can be captured, printed and ready for use in minutes.

Chapter 6

It all comes out in the wash: using TV 'soaps' with pupils who have learning disabilities

Vivian Hinchcliffe

Another workshop at the **Access to Learning** *Conference explored the uses of the ever-popular television drama format.*

> 'Blair Orders Deirdre Probe. Tony Blair was last night poised to step in and save Coronation Street's Deirdre Rachid from jail.'
> *The Sun*, 31 March 1998

> 'Millions celebrate as Deirdre is freed. Academics say 'emotionally correct' Britons are losing their sense of reality – to the extent that a TV drama becomes "true".'
> *The Daily Telegraph*, 17 April 1998

The distinction between fiction and reality can be fragile; drama lures many of us into what Bruner calls the 'narrative mode of thought', i.e., human acts of imagination. When I read these headlines, I immediately thought back to some early work we did under the curriculum area 'Personal and Social Cognition' (see Staff of Rectory Paddock School 1983). Some of our pupils with severe learning disabilities *genuinely* experienced (and many still do) difficulties with the fiction-reality distinction; they really did think that 'soaps' were real. We invited Tom Watt ('Lofty' from Eastenders) to visit school to accentuate the fiction-reality distinction. We briefed him to talk about the differences between the real life of Tom Watt the actor and the fictional character of 'Lofty' from Eastenders. By the end of the session, some of our pupils had a firmer grip on the fiction–reality distinction.

Fiction – reality distinction

Watching and discussing soaps is still an important part of the school's scheme of work in English. 'Soaps' are immensely popular; a large proportion of pupils watch them. The Australian 'soaps' screened at tea-time are often the most popular; however, many children watch the evening 'soaps' with their families. Whether we

'Soaps' and children's developing 'theories of mind'

like it or not, 'soaps' have become part of our cultural environment and they represent a medium through which we can explore both our own and other people's lives. Spend some time on a school playground and you will almost certainly hear children talking about 'soaps'. 'Soaps' are all around us as celebrities from them are on television, in magazines, on billboards, even singing in pop videos.

In school, we use video-recordings of episodes from 'soaps' for a variety of purposes. We use them for sequencing, using recent episodes to ask children what happened before, what happens next, which characters they like, dislike, and why. At a higher level, we focus on characters' mental states, i.e., their intentions, beliefs, desires and emotions. In developmental psychology, contemplation of people's mental states is called 'theory of mind' (Premack and Woodruff 1978). A theory of mind is a person's ability to infer people's mental states (beliefs, desires, intentions, emotions, imagination). All of us, most of the time, take account of what people think, believe, want, intend to do, imagine, etc., – it's a way of understanding and explaining people's behaviour.

Children's ability to appreciate and infer mental states is a critical milestone in their development. 'Soaps' represent a powerful medium in which to explore and discuss people's mental states because 'soaps' are particularly rich in what Bruner calls the 'landscape of consciousness' (Bruner 1986). This is what makes 'soaps' so popular, or unpopular. Bruner writes about two story landscapes on which narratives are based. One is the 'landscape of action' which contains the constituents of the action, i.e., the sequence of events , which Bruner likens to a 'story grammar', and the 'landscape of consciousness': what those involved in the action 'know, think, or feel, or do not know, think or feel', i.e., their psychological states.

Figure 6.1 shows categories of words about mental and personal properties. Watching and discussing characters' intentions, emotions, beliefs, etc., provides the teacher with rich opportunities to talk to pupils about the meanings of words relating to mental states.

Sections (A), (B) are self-explanatory. The words listed under section (C) *Perception Language* were included because our work revealed how difficult many pupils with learning disabilities found it to verbalise about perceptual experience. The metacognitive words listed in section (D) refer to states of knowledge or awareness (or the lack of them, e.g., forget, 'I don't know', 'I don't understand', etc.). Truth-value/Reality Language (E), is an important category because so many of our pupils find it difficult to 'take communications as cognitive objects and critically analyze them' (Flavell *et al.* 1981). Our ability to offer judgements about statements comes so easy to us in everyday speech that it is easy to overlook how difficult this is for many students with learning disabilities. Included under this heading are words relating to knowledge of the distinction between appearance and reality. The acquisition of such knowledge is, according to Flavell *et al.* (1983), 'a very important developmental problem... The distinction arises in a very large number and variety of ecologically significant cognitive situations. In many of these situations, the information available to us is insufficient or misleading, causing us to accept an apparent state of affairs (appearance) that differs from the true state of affairs (reality)...' Finally, under (F) *Metalinguistic Language*, we list words about language and some of its functions. Cazden (1983) defines metalinguistic knowledge or awareness as 'the ability to make language forms opaque and attend to them in and for themselves'.

(A) CHARACTER/BEHAVIOUR LANGUAGE: careful, careless, kind, unkind, generous, mean, polite, rude, friendly, gentle, lazy, helpful, greedy, patient, honest, cheerful, cruel, responsible, stubborn, thoughtful.

(B) ATTITUDE/EMOTION LANGUAGE: happy, pleased, glad, sad, unhappy, grateful, angry, cross, frightened, afraid, scared, worried, hope, look forward to, disappointed, excited, bored, sorry, ashamed, jealous, wish, proud, shy, embarrassed, lonely, fed up.

(C) PERCEPTION LANGUAGE: see, hear, smell, feel (physically), notice.

(D) METACOGNITIVE LANGUAGE: know, think, remember, forget, mean (intend), wish, hope, wonder, guess (English), believe, understand, be sure, expect, find out, idea, decide, make up mind, change mind.

(E) TRUTH-VALUE/REALITY LANGUAGE: right (a statement), true (a statement), wrong (a statement), pretend, mistake, dream, trick, joke, act, mean (speaker), story, really happen, not really happen.

(F) METALINGUISTIC LANGUAGE (incl. SPEECH ACTS): understand, mean (words), explain, argue, pretend, lie, ask, agree, promise, apologise, tell off, cheer up, remind, thank, persuade.

Figure 6.1 Vocabulary of target words about mental and personal properties

(From Hinchcliffe, V. and Roberts, M. (1987) Developing Social Cognition and Metacognition, in Smith, B., *Interactive Approaches to the Education of Children with Severe Learning Difficulties*.)

It can be safely assumed that pupils with severe learning disabilities will have delayed understanding of mental states. In attempting to develop children's awareness of the psychological world, teachers are faced with the problem that many psychological states (particularly metacognitive) deal with intangible entities, which cannot be directly perceived or demonstrated – intentions, beliefs, desires, feeling states, etc., (Hinchcliffe and Roberts 1987). However, most pupils with severe learning difficulties can be assumed to have experienced these things within themselves, at least in some rudimentary form. One of our aims of using 'soaps' is to make the children *consciously aware* of mental events and activities, both within themselves and, by analogy, within other people.

Hinchcliffe and Roberts (1987) analysed parental reports of the spontaneous language of a group of Down's Syndrome children aged between two and eleven years. The authors found a paucity of mental state language being used by the sample. Findings from a larger study of children with severe learning difficulties showed a similar poverty of internal state language (Hinchcliffe 1995). Certain teaching strategies were found to be effective in teaching 'target' internal state words, which were used to develop conscious awareness of mental events and feelings, as well as the ability to talk about them.

Figure 6.2 shows the 'landscape of consciousness' in one episode of 'Neighbours'. This episode is rich in metacognitive content, providing the teacher with the following opportunities to talk to pupils about the meanings of metacognitive words, for example those in category D of Figure 6.1 above. Words relating to *metacognition*, i.e., relating to states of knowledge and awareness, *perception* and *attitude and emotion* are shown in italics. 'Secret' and 'secretly' are metacognitive words – they mean that other people *do not know* about the secret.

Quiz: Hanna cheats in a quiz – *secretly* finding answers to questions in advance. Later she *feels guilty* and says *sorry*.

'Toady's Diet: Toady's supposed to be on a diet – he cheats by eating extra food by *secretly* ordering pizzas.

Aerobics Class: Toady goes to an aerobics class to ogle girls, he *pretends* to have fainted to get mouth-to-mouth resuscitation from Jo, a girl he fancies (the male instructor *suspects* what he's up to and makes out that he is going to give mouth-to-mouth).

Birthday Treat: It's Susan's birthday. For a birthday *surprise*, she's 'kidnapped' by her family and taken for a boat trip – she *didn't know* where they were taking her – she *couldn't see* as she was blindfolded. When they remove the blindfold, they *trick* her by showing her a tiny boat, instead of showing her the real boat.

Drug dealers: drug dealers meet in an open-air cafe. They *don't know* they are being watched by police.

Figure 6.2 Metacognitive elements in one episode of 'Neighbours'

(On a deserted road) Marlene and Helen break down in their car on the way to a market.

Marlene and Helen see an approaching car. Shane is on his way to the market to sell some things. He sees Marlene and Helen, stops, and takes them to the market.

(At the market) Marlene sees a mirror in one of Shane's boxes which she thinks once belonged to Lou (Cheryl and Lou's house was recently burgled). **What does Marlene think?**

(Later at the market) Marlene and Helen see Shane with a painting which they think once belonged to Cheryl and which was recently stolen from Cheryl and Lou's house. **Now what do they think?**

(At the market) Cheryl and Lou arrive at the market looking for Marlene and Helen. Cheryl sees someone carrying a ceramic pig (which they've obviously purchased), very similar to one which belonged to Lou, which was stolen from Cheryl and Lou's house. **What does Cheryl think?** (Answer: Cheryl thinks that Bianca may be the burglar, as she has for some time. She thinks that Bianca may have been supplying Marlene with goods to sell at the market).

(On the road in Shane's van) Marlene and Helen see Lou's jacket in the back of Shane's van. **What do they think?** Shane abandons Marlene and Helen and drives off quickly. **Why?**

Figure 6.3 A market scene in 'Neighbours'

Figure 6.3 shows events in a market scene in another episode of 'Neighbours'. Questions which explore characters' beliefs and intentions are highlighted in italics.

Watching and discussing 'soaps' may present the following opportunities for pupils and teachers. Relevant Programmes of Study references are provided in italics (DfE 1995):

- Retelling the sequence of the main events of the story, that is, relating what the main characters did and what they said. *(KS1 sp& l to describe events, observations and experiences; KS2 sp&l to identify and comment on key features of what they see and hear in a variety of media; KS2 sp&l to recall and re-present important features of a presentation.)*
- Discussing characters' behaviour in reference to their mental states, that is, their beliefs, desires, intentions and feelings, for example, offering possible reasons why characters acted in the ways they did, why they said the things that they did, what were their intentions, what they may have wanted, what they may have thought and how they may have felt. *(KS1 sp&l to give reasons for opinions and actions; KS1 sp&l Key Skills to use talk to develop their thinking and extend their ideas in the light of discussion; KS2 sp&l to use vocabulary and syntax that facilitate the communication of more complex meanings.)*

● Discussing, in relation to specific episodes, what may have gone before and predicting what may happen next. *(KS1 Sp&l to explore, develop and clarify ideas; to predict outcomes and discuss possibilities; KS2 sp&l to share ideas, insights and opinions.)*

● Generalising and relating some of the events in 'soaps' to real-life occurrences, for example, identifying episodes in pupils' own lives when they have acted in the same way as story characters and felt the same emotions. *(KS1&2 Sp&l as above.)*

● Using 'soaps' to engage pupils in drama, encouraging active participation in a re-run of the story narrative, to play the parts of the main characters *(KS1-4 Sp&l to participate in drama activities, improvisation and performances of varying kinds, using language appropriate to a role or situation…)* through drama to actively participate in a possible continuation of the story narrative, to improvise within the general story framework, along lines chosen by the students *(KS1-4 Sp &l as above).*

'Soaps' and conflict

'Soaps' are full of conflict (which adds to their appeal). Characters deceive each other, play tricks on people, avoid trouble by putting blame on other characters. Characters are shown to be jealous, envious and manipulative. Script editors writing 'soaps' regard conflict as an essential design criterion. In terms of child development, conflict is a powerful agent for learning. Judy Dunn's longitudinal observation of young children in the home identified certain types of domestic situation which seemed to accelerate children's learning about the social world, particularly their awareness of psychological states (Dunn 1991). Two of these conflict situations were:

● situations when children attempt to alter other people's psychological states, for example using teasing behaviour, persuading, comforting, helping and joking;

● contexts in which they try to avoid some kind of disapproval (from parents or siblings), including a) behaviour which deliberately thwarts others' intentions; b) children's excuses to evade trouble or punishment; and c) their fibs and lies.

Conflict is intrinsically engaging: unpacking the intentions, beliefs and feelings of characters from soaps is appealing to pupils. Themes from 'soaps' provide rich opportunities for follow-up drama (see Hinchcliffe 1995).

Constraints

'Soaps' contain a melee of action, often with strands of different plots intermingled together. To achieve maximum impact, television directors rarely let a scene run for more than two minutes, preferring to have a series of mini-plots switching from one social context to another. Consequently, there are few free-standing, coherent scenes in 'soaps': they all have interruption from other sub-plots. Some pupils with learning disabilities find differentiation of plots difficult. Teachers can get round this by fast-forwarding video episodes to allow continuity. Another potential problem is that understanding of characters' actions (what they say, what they do) and intentions (why they act as they do) is dependent upon background information, i.e., familiarity with characters' personas and knowledge of the plot. Pupils have really got to be 'soap' fans to understand characters' actions and motives. Fortunately, in my experience, most pupils are avid 'soap' viewers. This means that video-recordings of 'soaps' are best used fairly soon after they have been broadcast on television. Popular 'soaps' are screened every day and the plots move on rapidly. Using out-of-date videos can create confusion among some pupils with severe learning disabilities, as their current knowledge of the story line presents foreground-background difficulties.

Conclusion

'Soaps' are immensely popular with adults and children alike. They are rich in conflict and affect. Children's engagements with other people's emotional attitudes towards people, objects and events are seen to be building blocks for their understanding of mental states (Hobson 1993). 'Soaps' represent compelling media in which to talk to children with learning disabilities about their own and other people's mental states, i.e., their beliefs, desires, intentions, emotions and imagination. 'Soaps' are powerful stuff.

Chapter 7

Putting the vision into the 'telly'

Olga Miller

Olga Miller is RNIB Development Officer: Services for children with multiple disabilities. In this chapter she reflects on issues relating particularly to problems in processing visual information.

Television provides an immediately accessible and absorbing route into visual images. Children seem particularly engaged by it. But access at the press of a switch or button belies the complexity not only of the process of getting the image to appear on screen but of our ability as humans to perceive and interpret that image.

There are lots of questions about vision which we never usually think about. For instance, the retina at the back of our eyes is just a thin two dimensional membrane covered with light sensitive cells – yet the images we see around us are three dimensional. How do we come to gain an understanding of objects, which enables us to recognise familiar objects in different circumstances, even when parts are obscured or new parts added? Because we can usually take for granted that all this happens without us even consciously thinking about it and that we are all accessing these hidden visual abilities, there is not usually a problem. Watching television is just part of our visual repertoire.

However those of us who work with children who have learning difficulties can take none of these things for granted. Many children with severe learning difficulties or disabilities will have problems processing visual information. As part of a general developmental delay they may well be functioning within the early levels of visual development. Some of these children will also have an ocular condition, which means that in addition to their processing problems the image they receive on their retina will be distorted or impaired. Some children will have lenses prescribed to help their visual acuity and correct their long or short sight. This will help their visual experience to be clearer but they may still not be able to easily process the visual images presented to them.

However, it is important to know why children have had lenses prescribed. Using inappropriate lenses for a visual task will not only confuse but also visually frustrate a child who will generally respond by trying to remove their glasses – in any way they can.

It is not easy to identify those children with visual processing problems. Generally their eyes will seem unimpaired and there are no obvious signs of visual difficulty. On close observation there may well be some unusual visual behaviours. The child may turn their head at an odd angle or may seek to get very close to the television. All these unusual visual behaviours could well be masked by the child's learning difficulties. These may also manifest in atypical behaviour. The inter-relationship between vision and learning is so deep that it is sometimes impossible to disentangle them.

In order to maximise the visual potential of children with learning difficulties it is helpful to know a little about the way vision works and develops.

The eyes are part of the brain, they are literally its outposts and develop very early in gestation. Our ability to see is a learnt and dynamic process. Seeing is highly personal and is interrelated with not only our wellbeing but also our personality. From birth we respond to light and movement but clear vision also relies on our ability to perceive colour, texture and form. Gordon Dutton (1997) describes functional vision as relying on four components. These he identifies as:

- Discrimination – is something there?
- Resolution – what shape is it?
- Recognition – what is it?
- Understanding – what does it do?

In the beginning our form vision is limited. Babies are concerned with a near world. This nearness results in large images, which cover the retina. Broadly speaking the characteristics of early visual functioning work like this:

Early	Later
Preference for the familiar	Interest in novel stimuli
Viewing part of an object	Viewing whole object
Interest in simple items	Interest in complex items
Interest in large items	Interest in small items

Those children who exhibit visual processing problems are sometimes described as Cortically Visually Impaired. You will see this written down as CVI. They may well have particular needs. They often have a very short attention span and seem to 'see' very little. Their visual skills will vary from minute to minute. Their visual functioning is particularly poor in new environments or if they are tired or unwell. Their vision may also be affected by medication. Like all children they need good contrast and lighting in order to be able to maximise their visual skills. But most children with learning disabilities will not have been identified as having a cortical visual impairment. However, they may still demonstrate the same visual behaviours and needs. So how can teachers help?

We now know more about how vision works. In order to maximise access to visual material for the children we teach it is useful to think of two main stages in the visual processing of incoming information.

The first can be described as Low-level vision. This level of vision helps us survive and is independent of communication and language. Low-level vision includes our ability to perceive depth, the surface orientation of objects and their boundaries. This includes edge detection. We are also aware of colour, texture and motion in space. Higher-level vision draws on our experience and learning. Thus Higher-level vision builds on memory to enable us to recognise objects and people. Communication enables us to develop the language to 'name' what we see. Access to a range of experience links visual images to a wider world and sensory integration gives us the supplementary information to give substance to our visual world. Usually Low and High levels of vision are operating in tandem but for some children there may be more dependence on Low-levels of vision because they have not developed full access to the other aspects of visual development.

There are some assumptions we can make. For instance, for those children functioning in the early stages of development we can engage their interest by:

- keeping visual images simple and large;
- using lots of movement;
- repeating images;
- making sure the child can get close enough to visual material or images;
- using good contrast;
- making plenty of light (but non-glare) available either as task lighting or backlight (such as computer or television screens);
- using bright colours, especially red and yellow although white is effective for some children;
- linking visual images with tactile ones;
- using sound to reinforce the visual image;
- selectively introducing other sensory stimuli, but not too much at once.

If all this is beginning to sound like an advert for the 'Teletubbies' it is worth reflecting on the approaches that programme makers use when designing programmes for children. You will find that they usually adhere to the basics of vision. Cartoons are also a good example of visual images, which are designed using knowledge of how vision works. Age appropriateness is obviously an important consideration when choosing visually engaging material although the popularity of cartoons goes on into adulthood.

For those wishing to try a bit of experimental programme making there is much which can be done in the classroom with a good video camera and plenty of light.

Note: Sources of further information on visual stimulation are included in the Reference section of this book.

Chapter 8

Case Studies: innovative projects using television and video in the classroom

Carol Ouvry

Further research in schools in 1998 identified interesting examples of real practice, based on the rationale above, devised by teachers and completed in the school context. This chapter tells the story of eight such projects.

Many teachers have been using television programmes or video to enhance their teaching for several years, but may still be frustrated by the lack of relevant material, the time it takes to set up equipment for making or watching video, the lack of equipment or of the expertise needed to make best use of it. In this chapter examples are given of ways in which video has been used in schools to support different aspects of the curriculum.

The schools which contributed these examples had all sent representatives to the workshops and conference on the use of TV and video as a teaching resource described above. Subsequently, all the schools were contacted and asked about the ways in which TV and video were being used. From these, a small number have been selected to show a varied range of projects for a wide age and ability range. These schools are all special schools, and nearly all cater for pupils with severe or profound and multiple learning difficulties. One is a school for pupils with moderate learning difficulties. However, many of the projects are flexible enough to be appropriate for use with other ability levels, perhaps with a little adaptation.

Television programmes and both commercially-made and school-made videos were used in these projects. They were used in many different ways, some to be watched and provide motivation for related activities; some as a record of work done; some as an assessment tool; and some were made by the students who learnt about the process of making videos as well as the content of the video they made. In the examples described the reader will notice that some schools obviously have a range of sophisticated equipment, the expertise and, apparently, the time to use it, whereas other projects

Introduction

have been carried out with only the simplest resources which are to be found in all schools.

A very noticeable feature of all the examples is that it was the need of the pupils which prompted the use of video, whether this was to enhance access to curriculum subjects, to increase motivation and involvement in a topic, to provide relevant resources for a theme or subject or to learn some of the skills of video making. It was this specific need, of course, which determined the way in which the TV or video was used.

All projects were carefully planned as part of a learning experience which was firmly linked with the curriculum, assessment or recording of achievements. The use of TV or video was never considered to be merely entertainment, although clearly there is nearly always an element of entertainment and enjoyment in watching or making a video.

The Case Studies are highly individual, as befits such a diverse community, but they are all organised as follows:

- Nature of the project;
- Why we did it;
- What we used;
- How we did it;
- What the pupils did;
- The outcomes;
- Lessons learnt;
- Next steps.

Contributors have made many very useful comments in the section on 'Lessons Learnt'. Some are to do with planning the content; some about videoing techniques and some about the practical organisation involved in using video in schools, whether it be in the production process or in devising a learning resource. All are practical and aim to be helpful to those readers who are considering using TV or video in a systematic way for a particular purpose.

In the section describing the 'Next Steps', a number of approaches have been taken. Some people have considered how the same project could be re-run and made more effective in the future; some have thought of how the project could be extended and move on in terms of technical competence, content and format. Some have considered how use of video could be increased and used more regularly as a teaching method.

Despite the enormous differences in approach and purpose to which TV and video have been put, the enthusiasm which comes across in the following descriptions shows how useful and exciting the use of TV and video can be, and how it can trigger both practical and imaginative approaches to teaching.

I should like to acknowledge the work of the people who contributed these examples, and to thank them and their colleagues for agreeing to share their experience with the readers of this book. I am also very grateful to them for providing the information at one of the busiest times of the school year and, in some cases, spending time at the beginning of their hard-earned holidays to write up projects to send in time for them to be incorporated into this chapter.

Case Study acknowledgments

The nature of the project

This project was developed for pupils from five to twelve years old with profound and multiple learning difficulties.

In the project a 'Big Eye' projector was used to help to create special learning environments and sensory experiences so that pupils could participate in a meaningful way in a History and Geography scheme of work based on Robin Hood (See Appendix following this report).

The subject was introduced through a 'stimulus visit' to a local exhibition, watching videos and a visit to a local park.

Drama was the main method of working in school-based sessions but methods also included art and a presentation at assembly.

Case Study 1: The Life and Times of Robin Hood

Why we did it

This approach was used for a number of reasons. We felt that by projecting video images onto a large screen pupils with visual impairment might have greater access to visual experiences of history and geography. As pupils themselves were shown in the video we made, we hoped that this would increase the self-awareness and self-esteem of those who were at the early stages of personal development. Also, since the pupils concerned were at a pre-verbal level of communication, the life-sized moving pictorial images could provide alternatives to verbal approaches.

The project was seen as progression from the virtual environments created with concrete materials already used with these pupils, and a step forward towards a more abstract involvement and under-standing of their environment.

What we used

This project involved a number of different learning environments and a range of specialised equipment.

Environments
The visualisation room. This has white blinds and a whole range of special stimuli such as sound effects, smells, lighting effects, fog machine, bubble machine. The room is used to create a varied range of virtual environments.

Out of school environments including the 'Tales of Robin Hood' exhibition at Nottingham, and Wollaton Park – a local park and woodland.

Equipment
   Video camera for filming
   The Big Eye projector
   Large screen (8ft X 10ft)

Commercially-produced videos of Robin Hood. Two versions were used; one from about 20 years ago, the other a recent film.

How we did it

Week 1
Before we started the sessions in school, we all visited an exhibition 'The Tales of Robin Hood' in Nottingham. This visit was intended to set the scene for the following weeks.

The first part of the exhibition is a large screen video with voice-over showing Sherwood Forest as it would have been in the 11th century. At first the video shows the forest during the day, and gradually the moon comes up and evening falls. A door opens in the centre of the projected image and visitors walk through the door and back in time. The rest of the exhibition consists of simulated scenes of the typical life of peasants, outlaws and rich men.

Back in school we all watched a commercial video of Robin Hood. We wanted the pupils to become familiar with the tune 'Riding through the Glen' to be used in future sessions, and to watch the movement of people, and aspects of life in the 11th century.

Week 2
We first had a drama session on the early life of Robin Hood. Later in the week we went to Wollaton Park, where pupils made their own 15-minute video of deer moving around a woodland area in the park. Towards the end of the video pupils were also recorded in front of the deer and the woods.

Week 3
In the first session we converted the visualisation room to represent Nottingham Castle, dungeons and Sherwood Forest. The second session of the week was a dramatisation of the story of Robin Hood becoming an outlaw.

Week 4
The week started with a drama session based on the theme of 'taking from the rich and giving to the poor'. The theme of sharing was followed up in assembly later in the week.

The setting for the assembly was a large tree (a converted

wheelchair swing) positioned near the outside door with a sign saying 'THE MAJOR OAK'. The assembly leader talked about Robin Hood hiding in Sherwood Forest in the Major Oak (a historic tree in the forest) and asked 'How many people can hide in a tree trunk?' 12 pupils in wheelchairs went into the trunk of the 'Major Oak' and out of the back entrance.

A large screen video of Robin Hood in Sherwood Forest was then shown, followed by an activity on taking from the rich and giving to the poor, emphasising the moral that we should all share. Finally, the video with the Robin Hood song was shown, and everyone joined in with the singing.

The use of video in further sessions

Weeks 5 to 11 all consisted of a dramatisation of a character or event from the story of Robin Hood. (See Appendix 1 – Detailed Scheme of Work.)

Each session began in the Robin Hood visualisation room with the school video of the woods from Week 1 projected onto a whole wall. This provided pupils with a cue to the session and also set the scene for the activities that were to follow. After each of the sessions a different video of a story of Robin Hood was shown, and wherever possible this was related to the subject of the session.

The following is an example of the drama session in week 9:

All of the pupils were in the visualisation room with the home video projected onto the wall.

Adult: Let's think about what Robin Hood did when he wanted some food
He found some food in the forest – like raspberries. *All eat one.*
But sometimes he went to the market.
Let's make a medieval market.

The pupils and staff are put into groups with one adult to two pupils.

Adult: Each group can make a stall.

Each group sets up a stall with materials which are available on two large tables. Table 8.1 shows the organisation of this activity.

What the pupils did

Pupils watched a video of the 11th century at a 'Tales of Robin Hood' exhibition and walked through the door in the video screen into the past.

Group	Stall	Sight	Sound	Smell	Taste	Touch
Group 1	Pots, pans, brasses					
Group 2	Leather, sacking, wool					
Group 3	Eggs, milk, poultry					
Group 4	Herbs and potions					
Group 5	Vegetables and fruit					

Table 8.1 Stall organisation for a medieval market

- They participated in the process of making a 'school video' of woods and deer on the outside visit.
- They used the 'school video' as a weekly reminder of the sessions.
- They watched a short commercial video of Robin Hood with the whole school to focus and motivate during assembly.
- They took part in a series of drama sessions based on the legend of Robin Hood.

The outcomes

Stimulus visit to 'Tales of Robin Hood' exhibition
Pupil responses: All students responded positively. Pupils with visual impairments did look at the large screen. Walking through the door in the screen was an excellent virtual experience and pupils were all very alert and aware of things happening.

Making the school video of woods and deer
Pupil responses: Pupils showed by their facial expression and body language that they enjoyed the session. The video was of a very good quality and when shown through the Big Eye projector, images of deer and pupils were life-sized. Because of the pupils' communication needs it was not possible to know whether or not they associated the activity of making the video with the playback of it in school.

It appeared that the school video provided a sense of 'self' involvement in the project. Whilst students smiled when they entered the visualisation room and saw the video, staff also felt a strong sense of 'belonging' in the project.

Use of the school video in drama sessions
Pupil responses: At the beginning of each session the school video was shown in the visualization room with a range of simulated environments e.g. Nottingham Castle, the dungeons. This provided an atmospheric clue to the weekly sessions and pupils did appear to show anticipation for the forthcoming activities. Pupils who were able to communicate their feelings were alert and vibrant, and when asked 'Do you want to do Robin Hood?' the answer was 'Yes'.

Contribution to scheme of work
During sessions it was very useful to be able to point to relevant places on the video e.g. a large tree, a deer.

Use of the Commercial Robin Hood video
Pupil responses: The use of the large size videos of Robin Hood's adventures was particularly useful for both auditory and visual experiences. Horses galloping, swords clashing and arrows swishing held attention and many pupils showed signs of exhilaration and excitement during the videos.

The use of the videos alongside similar simulated experiences may have provided a link to aid pupils' understanding and awareness, but it was not possible to assess this.

Lessons learnt

It is essential to have a number of people who are able to operate video equipment and to have everything always ready beforehand. Searching for videos and setting up systems is time-consuming and can be very frustrating.

The school video was made at adult eye-level. In retrospect it should have been at the eye-level of the pupils in wheelchairs.

We now feel that with more careful planning we could have made videos in all the experience sessions, both as records of work, and to use as future teaching resources.

Next steps

After the successful use of video in these sessions, we now intend to make the use of video/TV an integral part of all planning.

At the present time a video club operates in school with only commercial videos, and we hope to extend the range to include videos made with and by pupils in the school.

The use of the Big Eye projector will be further explored in a number of ways such as using mirrors to create 2-sided virtual environments; providing quick change stage-sets for whole school drama productions; using screens with doors as in the 'Tales of Robin Hood' exhibition.

Virtual environments have been used in the school for a number of years now both in the form of special rooms and computer programs and these will continue to be extended by the use of video and TV.

Appendix 1 to Case Study 1

OVERVIEW OF SCHEME OF WORK	
Week	**Activity**
1	a) Stimulus visit to 'Tales of Robin Hood' exhibition b) Watch video of Robin Hood
2	a) Drama – The early life of Robin Hood b) Outside visit to Wollaton Park Make video of woods and deer
3	a) Art – convert visualisation room* to Nottingham Castle Dungeons Sherwood Forest area * The visualisation room has white blinds and a whole range of special effects can be used e.g. 600 sound effects; 30 smells; lighting effects; fog machine; bubble machine. The room is used to create an ongoing range of virtual environments. b) Drama – Robin becomes an outlaw
4	a) Drama – Taking from the rich – giving to the poor b) Assembly Video of Robin Hood Activities on the theme of 'sharing'
5	Drama – The forest
6	Drama – Alan-a-Dale
7	Drama- Will Scarlet
8	Drama – Maid Marion
9	Drama – Market Place – buying
10	Drama – Market Place – archery competition
11	Drama – Death of Robin Hood

Appendix 2 to Case Study 1

DETAILED SCHEME OF WORK FOR ROBIN HOOD		
Week	**Activity**	**Objectives**
Week 1	(a) Stimulus visit to 'Tales of Robin Hood' exhibition	• for pupils to experience and be visually aware of aspects of Sherwood Forest in 11th century. (History) • for pupils to be visually aware of woodland areas – the colour green, leaf movement, trees. (Geography) • to become familiar with the tune 'Riding through the glen'
	(b) Watch commercial video of Robin Hood	• to observe aspects of living in 11th century (History) • to watch movement of people from place to place e.g. from wood to market place, to castle (Geography)
Week 2	(a) Drama – the early life of Robin Hood	
	(b) Outside visit to Wollaton Park to make video of woods and deer	• for pupils to be involved in making a video of woods to use in future sessions • to enable pupils to remember the video of the woods seen in the exhibition and remember the visit from week to week by using their own video (History) • to give pupils the opportunity to visit a different environment in the locality of the school
Week 3	(a) Convert visualisation room to Nottingham Castle Dungeons Sherwood Forest area (b) Drama – Robin Hood becomes an outlaw	

Week 4	(a) Drama – taking from the rich and giving to the poor	• provide a strong focal point to gain motivation and attention
	(b) Assembly – video of Robin Hood – theme 'Sharing'	• provide an opportunity for the whole school to have some understanding of the person 'Robin Hood'
Week 5	Drama – The Forest	
Week 6	Drama – Alan-a-Dale	
Week 7	Drama – Will Scarlet	
Week 8	Drama – Maid Marion	
Week 9	Drama – Market Place *buying*	• for pupils to experience items from a mediaeval market • for pupils to have a range of sensory experiences • for pupils to fulfil their own individual educational objectives
Week 10	Drama – Market Place *archery competition*	
Week 11	Drama – Death of Robin Hood	

Case Study 2: All about us

Nature of the project

This project was part of the Personal and Social Education curriculum for a class of students in years 9 and 10 (14 and 15 years old) with severe or profound and multiple learning difficulties. In the sessions the students discussed themselves and their families, and videos were made at home and sent into school showing special cultural events, for example, a Bengali wedding.

Why we did it

A large number of students in this class group are Bengali, and they share many interests and cultural experiences. The whole school celebrates their festivals and this is always an exciting area of school life for all students. The following example draws on two sessions in which we used the video of a Bengali wedding.

What we used

Video film of the wedding reception of a Bengali member of staff.

How we did it

First of all we looked at pictures of families and discussed relationships, for example mum and dad, brothers and sisters, husbands and wives. We asked whether any of the class were married. The students found this funny, and sometimes embarrassing. We discovered which members of staff were married, and looked at wedding photographs of an English and a Bengali wedding. We then talked about the recent wedding and watched the video of the reception.

What the pupils did

Many of the pupils contributed to the discussion, talking about the different clothes and whether they thought people were happy or sad. They talked about whether they would like to get married.

Students with profound and multiple learning difficulties were given examples of the beautiful fabrics to handle, the perfume to smell, and listened to the music.

The outcomes

The video was clearly enjoyed by all the students who seemed to respond more to the fact that they could see people they knew, and that the bride was someone they saw every day, but in a very serious context.

Lessons learnt

Students respond more positively to video than photographs. The fact that the video had someone who they knew added to their interest. There were familiar elements in the situation, as all the students had attended some form of Bengali celebration in their past. Watching the video gave them an opportunity to reflect more on the meaning of the event.

Next steps

Nothing specific planned yet.

Nature of the Project

The study of National Curriculum English, Key Stage 3 – Shakespeare
   This project was carried out with a mixed ability group of pupils from 12 to 14 years with Severe Learning Difficulties or Profound and Multiple Learning Difficulties. Many of the pupils had severe communication difficulties and associated challenging behaviour.

Case Study 3:
English Literature:
The Tempest

Why we did it

This project was devised to support the delivery of National Curriculum English and to enable pupils to access a complex piece of literature through direct experiences involving visual aids and the experience of performing. We also wanted to produce a video record of the performance.

What we used

We used a wide range of resources including:

- a commercial video of 'The Tempest';
- written text adapted by the teacher;
- camera and photographs;
- video camera;
- a range of equipment for making props and sound effects including;
  echo machine
  musical instruments and drum machine
  voices of pupils for sound effects
  recorded music.

How we did it

At the start of the project the play was told as a story to the whole class and this was followed by the pupils watching a commercial video of the play.

In the following sessions parts of the play were acted out by the pupils and this also involved making props and using sound effects. For this particular project, the props we made were puppets, but in similar projects based on other literature sources the props have included scenery and other large and small items used in the production.

Each section which was performed was filmed, and the videos were used to analyse performances and talk about characters and emotions. A display for the school was made with photographs and drawings with written subtitles, and descriptions of the characters in the play.

Finally videos of the sessions were edited to form a single performance, and this was shown to the whole school.

What the pupils did

The pupils were involved in a wide range of activities and experiences, including:

- listening to and experiencing the 'story' and the commercial video;
- discussing the characters;
- making a chant on the drum machine, by using Shakespeare's words in a 'ditty' with rap music and signing;
- operating equipment. For example, they took photographs, filmed, used musical equipment. Pupils with PMLD used switches to operate keyboards, drum machine and sound effects;
- using their own voices which were recorded to make scary and eerie noises;
- dressing up and discussing the costumes;
- making props in Technology sessions;
- making decisions about editing the video film;
- showing the video of the performance to the rest of the school.

What the outcomes were:

The group was highly motivated throughout the project and there was evidence of learning in a number of different domains. The pupils:

- remembered the storyline, characters and the author;
- experienced and learnt about different equipment;
- valued each others' role in the production;
- all took part;
- had a great sense of achievement, and were proud of what they had produced;
- had ownership of the project.

Lessons learnt

- The project was time consuming, and more was planned than was actually achieved. It took a term to complete.
- The staff need more practice with the technology involved, and more practical use of the equipment.
- Collaboration is helpful. The music teacher contributed significantly. His input was invaluable.
- Pupils had to become aware of the need to be silent during recording.
- Better editing equipment is needed.
- Practice helps – this is the third project of this type done by S3 and it gets better and easier each time. Other projects of this type include *The Ancient Mariner* and *The Wind in the Willows.*

Next steps

More projects – possibly with a poetry content.

Nature of the project

Video was used for assessment with pupils in the primary department with profound and multiple learning difficulties or multisensory impairment. It was used in conjunction with the *Affective Communication Assessment* (*ACA*: Coupe and Goldbart 1987) as a backup for teacher observations in recording pupils' reactions and behaviour. The results were used for analysis and planning of individual education programmes in school.

Case Study 4:
Use of video to
support Affective
Communication
Assessment

Why we did it

We thought that video would be useful to help to identify communicative behaviour, and the stimuli and settings in which this behaviour was most likely to occur. It would help us to get a greater understanding of the individual pupils concerned, and also to assess functional vision and hearing. The results would be used to inform teaching and planning.

What we used

Environments: We used a variety of settings and activities both at home and at school.

Resources: video recorder; resonance board; variety of objects providing visual and auditory experiences; *Affective Communication Assessment* forms for recording responses.

How we did it

The teacher or carer observed the pupil to get a general idea of likes and dislikes in terms of the environment, activities and people. Videos were made at home and at school and staff and carers used these to try to identify different behaviours. In some instances the teacher went to the home and filmed the parents / carers working with the pupil. The videos were discussed with parents and staff who were involved in the assessment process.

The following is an example of one pupil who has profound learning disabilities and dual sensory impairment, who often appears unhappy and uncomfortable. Staff have found it difficult to identify the cause of her distress, and therefore to deal with it effectively, except by cuddling and maintaining physical contact with her. It was felt that her dual sensory loss might be causing feelings of extreme insecurity and a need for continual physical contact and reassurance.

Discussions with her parents and all the staff working with her in school helped to identify conditions in which she seemed most content, and these conditions were reproduced to assess her vision and hearing and to try to find an experience which she liked which could be used in future sessions to encourage interaction and communication.

In six separate sessions the pupil was presented with a variety of visual and auditory stimuli including fibre optic torch, colour torch, glowbug, tambour, chimes, guiro, shaker. The *ACA* record was completed by the teacher at each session. Two of the sessions were video filmed, and all of the classroom staff completed the *ACA* record from the videos of these two sessions. (See Appendix for example of the recording form.)

The results over the six sessions were compared, and records of the two videos made by individual staff members were also compared to reach a consensus of interpretation as to which responses indicated *like, dislike, indifference* or *preference*.

What the pupil did

The pupil showed clear reactions to auditory stimuli, but less so to visual stimuli, suggesting that she found stimuli through vision less rewarding than through her residual hearing. She showed clear dislike of some sounds (for example, chimes) and indicated this by grimacing and moaning. She showed clear stilling to sounds she liked and increased activity once the sound had stopped which the staff interpreted as a request for more of the sound.

The way the pupil reacted at home and in school gave a clear idea of the optimum conditions in which she would respond – a quiet environment, no body brace, lying down, with a familiar adult, with hearing aids and a vibrotactile aid. (This is a small piece of equipment similar to a wristwatch which is sensitive to sound.) Through this the pupil was able to *feel* speech, and therefore needed less direct physical contact.

The outcomes

Consistent responses were identified, e.g. stilling, increased leg movement.

Favourite sounds were identified. These sounds have been incorporated into some 'intensive interaction' sessions which have also been filmed. This has allowed other staff and carers to see how she is responding in these sessions.

In general, video has turned out to be most important as a means of raising awareness in members of staff who do not know the pupils so well. By watching the videos with staff who do know the pupils well, they have been able to see how a child is reacting, and this has led to greater understanding of the pupil's needs and communicative behaviour by staff and carers. As a group, the staff are now responding more consistently to pupils, and providing a more predictable environment.

Lessons learnt

- Setting up a video camera in a busy classroom and providing optimum conditions for carrying out a valid *Affective Communication Assessment* is difficult.
- Prioritising a number of sessions (at least six) to work on responses to visual and auditory stimuli and recording two of these allowed for consistent responses and valid observations to be made.

● It was extremely useful to use information from observations made at home and at school to identify general likes, dislikes and communicative behaviours.

Next steps

Continue to use the video for observation purposes, especially with the increasing amount of intensive interaction being undertaken.

Appendix to Case Study 4

ACA OBSERVATION Recording Sheet		STIMULI								DATE:				
CHILD'S NAME														
HEAD	Turn – R/L. U/L													
	Activity													
	Rotating													
	Other													
FACE	Frown													
	Smile													
	Anguish													
MOUTH	Activity													
	Open/close													
	Tongue activity													
	Contact													
EYES	Activity													
	Open/close													
	Gaze													
	Localise/search													
HANDS	Activity													
	Finger activity													
	Contact													
ARMS	Reaching													
	Activity													
LEGS	Activity													
BODY	Activity													
VOCALISATION	Utterance													
	Cry													
	Laugh													
	Other													
	AFFECTIVE COMMUNICATION Interpretation of child's behaviour													

ACA OBSERVATION Recording Sheet	STIMULI								DATE:					
CHILD'S NAME:														
AFFECTIVE COMMUNICATION Interpretation of child's behaviour														

DATE: _____
CHILD'S NAME: _____

ACA SUMMARY SHEET

STIMULUS	AFFECTIVE COMMUNICATION (Adult's interpretation)	REPERTOIRES OF CHILD BEHAVIOURS	ADULT INTERACTION	RESULTS

Case Study 5: Animation

Nature of the project

This project was part of a cross curricular topic approach to address the National Curriculum foundation subjects. The topic 'Animation' included activities in many subject areas, but had Art as the main focus.

Why we did it

The school plans half termly topics in departments to address the foundation subjects within the national curriculum. Each topic has a different main subject focus. Planning ensures that a 'broad and balanced' curriculum is delivered, which addresses all areas of the programmes of study. Differentiation of the content of activities ensures equal access to the curriculum for all pupils regardless of age or ability.

This topic addressed elements of the Art curriculum. Many pupils with learning difficulties find the TV, animation and sound particularly captivating. Familiar characters, stories and music were chosen as starting points for many of the activities.

The project was devised for pupils in the middle school aged 12 to 16 years. All pupils have severe learning difficulties or profound and multiple learning difficulties, and many of them have physical impairments in addition to their learning difficulties.

What we did

The topic was carried out through all subject sessions (see Appendix 1, Topic Plotter). Activities included:

- visits to the Disney shop, to the cinema/children's world, and a visit to the school by a popular cartoon character;
- making three dimensional models from plaster of Paris;
- cooking a variety of foods related to cartoons and cinema;
- stories associated with pupils' favourite cartoon characters;
- role-play involving face painting and masks;
- making cartoon character masks and then a giant model of one cartoon character;
- watching cartoon videos and black and white video of 'Watch with Mother';
- becoming familiar with cartoon jingles and film songs.

A Topic Planner for each subject (see Appendix 2) shows the detailed planning of the activities for each curriculum area.

The cartoon characters used were chosen in discussion with the members of staff who would actually be delivering the project. They were based on what the staff felt was appropriate in terms of the age of the pupils and their interests.

The outcomes

This topic was most successful with the less able of our SLD pupils and the pupils with PMLD. Using well known characters in cartoons and films was an effective starting point as pupils were familiar with them straight away.

The cookery elements worked well. Pupils recognised the characters and were motivated by this recognition to participate in the activity, e.g. opening the packets in the ready-mix cake box. The cookery activities proved effective in the development of body awareness, including the position of facial features. Good choice-making (D&T) activities.

Drama activities were also successful in that pupils recognised characters and many were keen to have their faces painted and have a go at painting each other's face! Good body awareness activities.

Pupils responded positively to music and stories they recognised, and were again motivated to participate and move to the music.

The available RE videos were not as motivating as other cartoon videos. They tended to have more subtlety in their presentation.

English story books, videos and story tapes appropriate to the age and stage of pupils were enjoyed by all classes.

Lessons learnt

- Videos chosen for use need to be in a format where the animation is bright and bold, with a simple accompanying text and/or lively or contrasting music to captivate pupil interest.
- Familiar characters were found to promote participation in activities across the curriculum.
- The animation topic presented good opportunities for 'body awareness' work.

Next steps

The topic is in a three year topic cycle so the next time it is visited the staff will review its suitability for the pupils in the classes at the time. The RE section will be reconsidered and possibly different videos used. Characters will be chosen which are relevant to current trends and popular favourites.

Appendix 1 to Case Study 5: Topic plotter

Topic – Animation Focus – Art
Department – Middle School
1st half of Summer term

	1	2	3	4
Visit	Disney Shop	Visit to school by popular cartoon character	Cinema/Children's world	
Science	Making 3D models from plaster-of-Paris			
English	Stories and jingles associated with pupils' favourite cartoon characters			
Drama	Role-play involving face-painting and masks			
Geography	Skills associated with visits			
History	Watch the black and white video 'Watch with Mother' (BBC)			
Art & Craft	Cartoon character masks		Giant model of one cartoon character	
Design & Technology	Face Painting in conjunction with Drama			
Food/Home Technology	Disney Cakes	Face Biscuits	Popcorn and Milkshakes	Pizza Faces
Music	Cartoon jingles and cartoon/film songs			
RE	Watch videos of animated Bible stories			

Appendix 2 to Case Study 5: Topic planner

Topic – Animation
Department – Middle School
Summer 1/2

Ref. no	Curriculum Area	Activity	Aims and Objectives	Organisation Strategies	Resources
1	Cookery	Disney Cakes	Pupils will be given a packet of 'Disney character' cakes. They will open the packets and with help make the cakes.	Work around the tables in the cookery room. Eat in lounge.	Pack of cake mixture.
2	Cookery	Face biscuits	Pupils will be given plain round biscuits. They will help to mix icing sugar and will be given a variety of coloured sweets. Each pupil will design their own 'Disney' face.	Work around the tables in the cookery room. Eat in lounge.	Biscuits, icing sugar, variety of sweets.
3	Cookery	Popcorn and Milkshakes	The pupils will make, as independently as possible, popcorn in the microwave. They will also choose a flavour of milkshake and make it.	Work around the tables in the cookery room. Eat in lounge.	Pop corn, milk flavourings.
4	Cookery	Pizza faces	Each pupil will be given a small pizza base, pizza sauce and a variety of toppings. They will choose their own topping & design a 'Disney' face.	Work around the tables in the cookery room. Eat in lounge.	Pizza base, pizza sauce, variety of toppings.

Topic planner

Focus: ARY

Topic/Theme – Animation
Department – Middle School
Term – 1st ½ School Term

Activity ref. number	Curriculum Area	Activity	Aims and Objectives	Organisational Strategies	Resources
Music	Music NC KS1 English S.C. and N.C. Listening Skills.	1. Watch sections of video (number of different characters introduced at a pace to suit the group) in which music is played in association with a character. 2. Listen to the music alone. 3. Match a picture of the character to the music.	1. To encourage listening skills. 2. To encourage visual attention to the screen. 3. To encourage the association of music with a character. 4. To assess pupil ability to match music to character.	Group activity led by teacher with other adults in support.	Video T.V. Taped music Tape recorder. Pictures of charaters.
Music/Drama	Music NC KS1 English S.C. and N.C. Listening Skills.	To use music associated with the characters as part of the drama lessons (particularly with the V.I. pupils).	See Drama plans.	Group activity led by teacher with other adults in support.	Video T.V. Taped music Tape recorder. Pictures of characters.
History	N.C. History at K.S.1	To watch programmes from the 'Watch with Mother' video. To discuss, at an appropriate level, how these programmes are different to modern day cartoons/programmes.	1. To encourage pupils to identify differences in past and present children's TV e.g. black and white v colour pictures, characters then and now. Pointing to pictures of characters from the video.	Class activity around the TV with teacher led discussion.	Watch with Mother video (BBC).

TOPIC PLANNER – Class 10 1st ½ Summer Term '97 Topic/theme – 'Animation'

Ref. no.	Curriculum Area	Activity	Aims & Objectives	Organisational Strategies	Resources
Wks 1–4	English	Watching "Winnie-the-Pooh" & other Disney videos (Barney).	T31. follow stories with pictures. S31.1 – single channel attention.	classroom furniture arranged so that everyone can see T.V. clearly (hear clearly).	T.V. & video tape.
Wk 2–4	'Us Two' p.33 e.g. 'Furry Bear' Now we are 6 p. 47	participating in songs & rhymes associated with 'Winnie-the-Pooh' & other cartoons.	T21. – vocalize in response to speech – use Makaton signs (S2) – enjoy songs & try to join in.	pupils sitting in a circle on chairs.	guitar and percussion instruments, soft toy or puppet of W-t-P.
Wks 1–4	"	"Matching pairs" game using 'W-t-P' characters & other cartoons in model & picture form.	T1 – interact with adult. T4 – show recognition & respond appropriately to familiar pictures.	1:1 adult to pupil during I.P. sessions. Use clear, minimum vocabulary, stressing "same" & "different".	pairs of model & picture cartoon characters – bag or box.

TOPIC PLANNER – Class 10 Middle School. 1st ½ Summer Term '97 **Topic/theme** – 'Animation' Art focus

Ref. no.	Curriculum Area	Activity	Aims & Objectives	Organisational Strategies	Resources
Wk 1	Art & Craft	Make textured pictures of "Winnie-the-Pooh" characters	Art A.T.1 iii a): consider pictures (models) of (cartoon) animals A.T.2 iii c): experience paper tearing & paper collage, paper scrunching.	1:1 pupil to adult. Prepared outlines of pictures for pupils to choose from.	glue coloured tissue, paper brushes, models & pictures of W-t-P characters,
Wk 2	"		See Science activity		
Wk 3	"	Paint giant Winnie-the-Pooh	Art A.T.2 v. c): use tools compitable with the activity. viii d): participate individually on small section of large picture.	1:1 pupil to adult within a group context. Prepare large outline in advance.	paint brushes, sponges, aprons.

TOPIC PLANNER – 1st ½ Summer Term '97 **Topic/theme** – 'Animation'

Ref. no.	Curriculum Area	Activity	Aims & Objectives	Organisational Strategies	Resources
SCIENCE	Science T1 Stg 1.3 T3 St 1	making plaster of Paris models of cartoon characters, using moulds.	1. Work with tactile materials to develop touch. 2. Experience feeling/ manipulating solid & liquid materials with time to express responses.	Class group as part of a craft activity.	plaster of Paris Cartoon character moulds.
T3 – MATERIALS	T3 Stg 2 T3 St 3		3. Experience materials that change in shape and/or consistency. Use malleable creative materials 4. Experience a change in materials through the use of tools (MOULDS).	(models can later be painted in Art)	*Water & plaster become a creamy mixture which rapidly solidifies.
	T3 Stg 5 (P.O.S & Indiv. Objectives)		5. Explore the properties of materials – Produce new objects from a variety of materials – i.e. MODELS FROM PLASTER + WATER.		

TOPIC PLANNER –

Topic/theme – 'Animation'

Ref. no.	Curriculum Area	Activity	Aims & Objectives	Organisational Strategies	Resources
Wk 1–4	R.E.	Look at video of Bible story depicted in cartoons.	1. To listen & look at video. 2. To understand part of story & be able to answer a question about what they've seen.	Videos hired from Christian Bk Shop in Wyndham arcade Margert to organise.	Videos. T.V. & Video.

TOPIC PLANNER – Middle School 1st ½ Summer '97 Topic/theme – 'Animation' Art focus

Ref. no.	Curriculum Area	Activity	Aims & Objectives	Organisational Strategies	Resources
Wk 1	Drama	Face-painting: – imitating a variety of cartoon characters.	English T1 all stages: interact with adults " " pupils. Art A.T. 2 viii a):– co-operate with teacher in creative venture.	Middle school classes combined, in the hall. Some pupils will be 'painted' while others watch.	face paints tissues, mirrors, cartoon - character - pictures & posters.
Wk 2	"	Role-play of "Mr Men" & "Little Miss" characters.	English T2 all stages: say 'Yes'/ 'No' or express by other means. T3 all stages: respond to instructions listen to stories.	as above. More able pupils will be encouraged to take a lead.	props & costumes. Mr Men jingles on tape.
Wk 3	as for wk 1 (different pupils to be painted)				
Wk 4	" " " 2 (different characters)				

Case Study 6: St. Francis and the natural world

Nature of the project

This was a Religious Education project, carried out with Year 9 pupils with Moderate Learning Difficulties in a special school. The project promoted understanding of the teaching of St. Francis and enhanced spiritual development by encouraging pupils to look closely at the natural world around them. Pupils learnt about the way in which St. Francis saw all living things as equal, calling trees, plants, animals and water 'Brother' and 'Sister'. By using video to record the beauty of the natural world, our pupils became more aware of their surroundings.

Why we did it

St. Francis' teachings can seem very separate from our pupils' lives. Most of our pupils live in a suburban area and many do not have a natural affinity with the countryside. By using the natural environment around our school – fields, the school pond, and flower beds, pupils were encouraged to see St. Francis' message of love and concern for the environment as being relevant for them.

What we used

Environments: Natural locations in and around the school including fields, the school pond and flower beds.
  Equipment: video camera; still camera; natural subjects – places, animals, plants, sky.

What we did

We began with a question – 'Who or what did we love in life?' Our pupils made a list, many talking about family or loved ones who had died. We then considered a more focused question 'Was it possible to love the world, and what would that mean?' Many pupils talked about care for the environment and trying not to pollute the world.

> Praised be my Lord for our mother the earth, which doth sustain us and keep us, and bringeth forth divers fruit and flowers of many colours and grass ... (Canticle to the Sun, St. Francis of Assisi 1181–1226).

We read the beautiful poetic prayer attributed to St. Francis, 'Canticle to the Sun', and discussed how every living thing, whether the sun or moon, animal or bird, plant or tree, was considered a Brother or Sister to the saint. We talked about what this would mean if we treated the world like this.

The class split into two groups: a photography group which would take stills for the school web-site, and a video group which would make a pop video. The video group was told to film the special natural places around the school which St. Francis would find beautiful. Could they find examples of his 'Brothers and Sisters'? This group was given a short lesson on how to hold the video, how to zoom in and out of the subject, and how to pan across.

The pupils clearly had remembered the Canticle to the Sun, and came back with assorted images of trees, a spider's web, puddles on the ground and many close-ups of flowers. There were also unexpected images that showed pupils were connecting with the idea; the school drinking fountain, a horse in a nearby field, and a film of clouds moving. As we watched the video, we turned down the sound and tried playing different pieces of music in the background. A teacher had a tape of classical music, and we tried different tracks from the cassette, such as Vivaldi's Four Seasons.

The quality of filming was variable. Some focused well on a subject, others moved the camera around. Some pupils with difficulties with motor skills had problems holding the camera still. The fast-moving sequences, rather than spoiling the film, were fascinating in their own way. For example, one pupil filmed up into a tree and moved the camera about quickly, so that the screen was a blur of different green. One boy said that the fast-moving images reminded him of modern 'Garage music' with the spiky, insistent rhythms.

We then decided to make a pop video, which was divided into two parts. The first section would use the calmer, more still images with a classical music background, and the second part would use the unfocused, hurried images, with a garage music background. The pupils decided which images would best suit the two sections and edited the video themselves, transferring images from the VHS-C cassette to the VHS video recorder.

A small group decided to make 'titles' for the video. They chose their own title which was interestingly, 'God is Love'. They then drew the titles on A4 paper, and disappeared with the video camera and sheets. They decided to fix the titles on different backgrounds, trying out different ideas and choosing the best one. The title sheets were filmed in bushes, on the grass, and against trees. This gave a very interesting effect and was the pupils' own idea. The titles were then edited into the final video.

The outcomes

At the end of the project, we had a lively pop video which conveyed the spirit of St. Francis's teaching and the philosophy of love for the world. However, what was important was the process that led to this outcome. Pupils had to evaluate what images would link with St. Francis's view of the world, rather than just filming what they wanted. It was clear that they were making aesthetic decisions as well – many enjoyed choosing the most bright and beautiful plants to film.

The interesting and exciting images brought back by pupils who found filming more difficult also gave a different slant to the project. We were able to incorporate the blurred and shaky images into the film, rather than rejecting them as 'wrong'. In a project about loving the world, this gave a clear message about inclusion, and valuing all of humanity.

The incorporation of the pupils' own music for the background, rather than the teacher's choice, encouraged a feeling of ownership of the final film. This pop video will now be used as a stimulus for pupils who begin their work on St. Francis. It has also been shown to teachers as part of training sessions on spiritual development in schools.

Lessons learnt

It was clear that it would have been a mistake to over-structure this project. It would have been easy to give pupils a 'shopping list' of shots to film. However, after talking about St. Francis' view of the world, they seemed happy and prepared to choose their own images to film, without teacher intervention. I feel that the selection of images was a key part of the project. Equally, it was interesting to hear the pupils' own soundtrack on the initial footage – some were doing a running commentary and explaining that they were filming 'Brother Sky' and 'Sister Water'.

Some pupils obviously needed more initial practice with using the video camera. Perhaps a longer training session would be appropriate in future.

Pupils obviously needed more guidelines on how long a shot should be, for example, learning to count to ten slowly while filming.

Next steps

Perhaps we could develop the project, looking at how we could convey more complicated ideas with video. How could we show 'Brother Fire' for example? Perhaps we could explore filming images from magazines.

Equally, some pupils were keen to produce their own documentary programme, interviewing teachers and pupils about their thoughts on pollution and the environment. This would need the teaching of more specific video skills, such as how to set up a studio type interview.

Nature of the project

The project was to devise and develop a sensory pack with a water theme for use with secondary aged students with profound and multiple learning difficulties. The pack was planned so that it could be used either at the swimming pool or in a 'dry' location, in which case a video would simulate the underwater experience.

Why we did it

At the time, there was a gap in the curriculum for activities specifically designed for students with PMLD. There was an identified need for these students to have access to an activity which could be repeated on a weekly basis for a period of time such as a term, in order to develop anticipation, communication and visual and auditory skills.

What we did

A whole school in-service training day was held, focusing on the development of sensory packs, and our group developed the idea of a theme around water. We decided to produce a pack which would provide a multisensory experience for a group of students with PMLD, within a cooperative and interactive environment.

What we used

Music relating to different aspects of the journey; video films; video with edited extracts to produce visual effects; props appropriate to each section of the activity, for example:

shells; seaweed (spaghetti); salt; bubbles; torches; fan and card; fans; bells and tambourines; water spray.

Case Study 7: Underwater experience for pupils with Profound and Multiple Learning Difficulties

How we did it

The theme was already agreed. We then wrote out a story line including songs, with three sections:

- on the beach;
- on the boat;
- under the sea.

We made lists of resources for each section (See the Appendix to this chapter) and collected clips of films which could represent water. These clips were then edited to produce a 'water video'

What the pupils did

The pack was mainly developed by the staff, but pupils participated in the process by making sea creature props with members of the staff. The appendix gives a detailed plan of how the activity was carried out, and what the staff and pupils did in each section.

The outcomes

We produced a multisensory pack which was well used and thoroughly enjoyed by both staff and students. (Appendix)

All pupils who participated in the sessions showed a positive response. This ranged from tolerance of handling to showing anticipation over a number of weeks.

Lessons learnt

- The bigger the TV screen and the smaller the group, the better.
- Repetition is extremely important for all students. It helps develop anticipative skills. We can monitor consistent responses to build up a profile of likes and dislikes and preferences for specific activities.
- Always have all the props ready before starting the session!

Next steps

Sensory packs are used a great deal in the school, although this is the only one which uses video/TV as part of the pack.

We will develop use of video in making sensory packs in the future.

Appendix to Case Study 7

Underwater Experience

Aims
To provide a multisensory experience for all students participating but in particular, those with PMLD.
   To create a cooperative and interactive environment

Group size
Maximum eight students (four in swimming pool)
One coordinator
Five adults (dependent on group)

Description
There are three sections to the 'Underwater Experience'
A – On the beach
B – On the boat
C – Under the sea

Each section is divided into three areas; resources, activity (inc. narrative) and song words.
   (Italics in the activity section denote cues if the pack is used in the swimming pool.)

Resource Checklist

In the Swimming Pool	*On Dry Land*
Tubs of sand	Tubs of sand
Salt to taste	Salt to taste
Star fish	Star fish
Box of sea shells	Box of sea shells
Seaweed	Seaweed (Spaghetti)
Water spray	Water spray
Fan and card for wind effects	Fan and card for wind effects
Bubbles	Bubbles
Audio tape of underwater experience	Video of 'Underwater Experience'
Audio tape of sea shore music	Audio tape of sea shore music
Percussion instruments (cymbals, tambourines,	Percussion instruments (cymbals,
tambourines, bells, drums).	bells, drums)
	Blue sheet
Tape recorder	TV and video
	Mats

A – On the Beach

Resources

Sand
Shells (big and small)
Seaweed (Spaghetti)
Salt to taste

Activity

- *(Done outside the swimming pool with students in chairs)*

- Narrator informs students that they are at the seaside and lets them feel the sand, shells and seaweed. Let them taste the salt.
- Lights are dimmed and sun with torch behind it is waved in front of students.
- Everyone joins in with Beatles song: 'Here comes the Sun'.

B – On the Boat

Resources

Water spray for rain
Fan and card for wind
Percussion instruments to create a storm

Activity

- Narrator informs students that they are going on a ride on the water in a boat. *(Students are lifted into pool one by one.)*
- They are rocked and swayed to the rhythm of the water.
- Rod Stewart's 'We are Sailing' is sung by everyone.
- After the song, the wind seems to be getting louder and stronger.
- Pupils are bounced and rocked, picked up and dropped in the ever stormy waters.
- Percussion instruments are banged.
- At the climax of the storm everyone screams 'Oh no we're sinking!'

C – Under the Water

Resources

Bubbles
Torches
Fans
Bells
Tambourines

Activity

- Pupils are rocked and swayed from side to side as they get deeper and deeper.
  'It's peaceful and relaxing under the sea.'
- Everyone sings Beatles' song: 'Octopus's Garden'.
- Everyone is getting tired and they decide it's time to go home.
- Everyone swims up to the surface.
- The adventure ends with everyone back on the beach listening to the seagulls.
  (One by one each student will be lifted out of the pool).

Nature of project

In this project I produced a multi-media careers resource for students with severe learning difficulties to be used with students from year 9 and to help them with post 16 Options at the school.

Why we did it

The Careers Library Initiative, funded by the then Wakefield Careers Service, offers a sum of money every year to purchase careers information resources. This is very helpful for mainstream pupils, but I soon found that there is very little available that is truly accessible by students with severe learning difficulties, so I decided to make our own materials.

What we used

486 PC computer with 8 mb RAM
RM multimedia authoring software – *Illuminatus*
Canon Ion digital camera plus videoblaster 200
Video camera
Clipart and sound collections
Tape recorder and microphone.

What we did

We devised and used a multimedia resource. I first chose the theme – what the options are for a 16 year old student at Park School. I had identified a lack of suitable careers resources. Mainstream careers material helps students make choices about their future. Students with severe learning difficulties have few choices, and in some cases don't get the opportunity to have a say in their future provision because adults make the choices for them. I wanted the students to see, through the use of photographs and video, what was on offer to them. I hoped that this would encourage students to voice their opinions as to placement post-16.

How we did it

I planned a storyboard on paper, i.e. what each page would contain. The title page has two pre-16 students at the centre and 7 buttons around them (see Figure 8.1). My voice says 'click a button to choose where to go'. Clicking the button activates my voice speaking the choice that the pupil has selected. Each button then takes the user to a new page containing a variety of photographs and video clips about that choice.

Progression Options for Park School Leavers

Adult Training Centre

Who Can Help Me Decide?

Stay at Home

QUIT

Residential College

Stay at School

Wakefield District College

Figure 8.1 Title page of story board

Each page was then planned.

I gathered necessary video clips, still photos and voiceovers. These were put together on a computer to run like a book; arrows to turn pages backwards and forwards; 'hot spots' behind graphics and photographs to take the user further into the book to more video and photographs. I found that the possibilities for video and photographs or text are endless. We could have branched and branched!

What the pupils did

The pupils posed in a variety of activities that they normally follow in all parts of Wakefield – out in the community, at college and at school.

The options available for our students are:

- to stay at home;
- to go to an Adult Training Centre;
- to go to a residential college;
- to go to Wakefield District College;
- to stay at school until 19.

I had photographs, clipart and video at each option, and then branched further within each one. For example, the 'Stay at School' option showed photos and video of students doing work experience, independent travel, independent shopping, college link courses and the ASDAN Youth Award Scheme which forms the basis of the Post 16 Curriculum. Voiceovers by the students in activities such as work experience, were also used.

The outcomes

A very useable multimedia resource was produced, which appealed to students because they knew the people shown in it. For example, in the Adult Training Centre video clip they could recognise a student who had left Park School two years previously. This makes the 'options' realistic and achievable. The resource contains voiceovers, titles and text, photographs, videos, music and clipart.

Lessons learnt

- Allow plenty of time to collect appropriate photographs, video clips and voice overs. Multiply whatever time you think you need by three!
- Aim for quality. It is important to get the best quality video and materials possible. I found that we had to revisit locations to re-record to improve the quality.
- Make sure that you have permission from students and any other people and places that you video.

- Have a clear storyboard and stick to it. This project could have branched on and on with more photographs and videos behind 'hot spots' on every page. Keep the page layout clear and uncluttered, yet attractive and exciting.

Next steps

At present I am negotiating with Careersoft to market this resource, or something similar. I would like to include Rebus with the next edition.

Time is always an issue, but I would like to do a similar project to inform students about the Youth Award Scheme modules, or Transition Teams.

Chapter 9

Communicating and creating with symbols

Nick Peacey and Tina Detheridge

The use of symbols as a support for language development and an expressive tool of communication has developed considerably in recent years. In this chapter, based on an interview between Nick Peacey and Tina Dethridge of Widget Software, the discussion examines what the impact of symbols may be in the future.

N.P. How is symbol use developing?

T.D. There are two fundamental ways in which symbol use is developing. The first is with people for whom text is unlikely to become a very useful means of written communication. What we are seeing with that community are people who have no expectations to write becoming readers and writers. The most dramatic examples are in the adult population. Anybody who has severe learning difficulties over the age of 40 has not been to school for sufficiently long to actually have what we would class as an education.

We are seeing 60 year olds coming along who, because of the help of technology are beginning to be able to write by selecting symbols on a board or clicking on a mouse or a touch screen.

They are beginning to communicate ideas, opinions and taking some real initiative. One lovely example was in some residential homes in a London borough who put a computer in each house. Previously care staff used to make the rotas. Because they can use a concept keyboard to choose them, the residents themselves are making the rotas. They are arguing with each other about whose turn it is to empty the bins and do the chores and the care staff don't get a look in. Now this is actually the kind of independence and autonomy that we have been talking about.

The next thing is that they start writing letters: they write letters back to their families; they write stories; they write about things they've been doing; they write diaries. So, as elderly people, they are becoming literate.

What we want to do is make sure that our young children start this at an early enough age. If you can suddenly do it at 60, I see no reason why you can't suddenly do it at 12 or 8 or 5! The most dramatic thing is this change of expectation.

The other area where there is a big change, I think, is in younger children. We see an interesting thing in the non-speaking population who have been used to using communication aids, have been doing face-to-face speaking and listening types of things, but who have not been looking at literacy. They haven't had a linguistic structure capability.

As they now start to want to explore things like poetry and literature, they realise the kinds of symbols they've used are not adequate for the job, so we are now having to radically rethink what symbols are. A picture of a boat is no good if you want to start talking about qualities of sailing and you want to talk about your emotions in connection with sailing, or about your imagination. We're needing to stretch the words we provide as symbols.

We have *Bliss* which is a language. It has all the qualities of a language, but that's too abstract for a lot of our users. We need something that is pictorially based but will allow them to move forward.

Our job as software developers is to make tools. We are not linguists; we are teachers. We are fundamentally interested but we are not experts. I'm not sure that there are experts because it's all so new. What we need to do is to make tools that people can explore and experiment with. We need a community of teachers/practitioners who are not afraid to experiment, who are not afraid to do things that are daft! Kids don't mind at all and you won't actually do any permanent damage to the child by messing with symbols! I think there are some professionals who are very protective; actually all kids are very resilient.

One of the examples is speech synthesis: teachers will say 'Oh we can't use that speech synthesis – it's too American' or 'it doesn't speak nicely.' If you listen to all the voices on cartoons kids listen to these days, day in, day out, and have no trouble decoding, you ask yourself why we agonise about the quality of a speech synthesiser. I think we need to get a bit of reality into all of this.

N.P. Are there projects you've seen developing or things that you can see coming up that you think are going to be relevant to the whole process of the development of symbols you've talked about?

T.D. One of the really important things about any kind of communication is that it is natural and normal. Signing for example, is very much kept within special schools or the private world, we haven't got signing as a normal linguistic element, even though we all use our hands and gesture. We have the same thing with symbols. When symbols were restricted to the walls of the special school, it was never a language. Even though we have symbols in every airport, every street, every motorway, somehow we've not made a connection: 'Actually those are the same things our kids use to read and write with.'

Somehow what we want to do is give it that kind of 'ordinariness' so that we see symbols around everywhere and everybody treats this as a normal means of communication. So for me, something like television is absolutely crucial because it is normal, part of everybody's culture. It's not different or separate. If we can just start having key symbols, in the same way as we use the symbols such as the suitcase indicating where to go and get your baggage. We could have key symbols on the screen at certain points to say 'This is what we're talking about'. This would achieve two things: a) it clues you into meaning and b) it just does that bit of making symbols normal and part of everyday life. It familiarises the whole of society with symbols so that then they are ready and conditioned when we want to look at more symbols on paper-based materials.

N.P. What's the role of education in moving children and young people from being watchers of television or other media into being active authors through symbols?

T.D. It's actually very easy, you just get them to write! One of the real problems with reading resources is age mismatch. Almost all of the literature/ early reading books are aimed at very young children and there is very little that is appropriate in interest to older readers. An eight year old who is a beginner reader is having to read still very much the *Wellington Square* type things. Every child has in them a million stories and so much creativity and two year olds will tell their parents wonderful stories taken from the stories that are read to them and their own experiences. What we want to do is to capture that as early as possible, rather than having to wait until you can decode text and you can form letters with pencil. For some children, they will have lost that whole imaginative fix and creativity. So my feeling is that children should be writers from the very first moment they can hold a pencil, click a mouse button or whatever. This again is where technology is brilliant because you can just click mouse buttons, click on pictures, sequence them and that's your story. Maybe the story is simply about somebody getting in a car and going somewhere silly. Maybe it's only five pictures, but so what!

The other thing that we've seen a lot of is using children's stories. There's a wonderful teacher in Sussex who does this; she gets children to write short stories just about their experience, being in the playground, going home, watching telly, what they saw yesterday. She helps them write it, using symbols and words in whatever mixture and then she takes that writing and she uses it for what the strategy calls literacy and what I call language work. She will say, let's go through it and let's find the nouns, let's find the verbs, let's find the *ons* and the *unders*, let's find all the words with magic 'e's in. So by starting with their story they're tuned in and keyed into the subject matter because it's theirs. We see an engagement that isn't there with external text. I actually think that getting kids to be writers and then using that writing for a structured underpinning of the grammatical aspect is a really powerful motivating thing.

We had a lovely project we did at Westminster College where we got teenagers writing stories for other teenagers. Of course they were writing about the things that teenagers want to write about, not what adults *think* teenagers want to write about. So that we've got things about 'The Day Gran Died' which is about what happens when somebody dies, what do you feel, what goes on, things that are quite difficult to talk about. We've got the story about the girl who wanted to have her nose pierced and her mum wouldn't let her, what happened, what was the family compromise, ordinary things that actually interest teenagers.

So I think actually getting kids to author for other children is absolutely brilliant. It does a lot for them as writers because their status goes up – 'I'm an important author'. It gives the reader two things: it gives them something to read but also a feeling that they could also become an author.

Because books normally are in hard cover, they're things you buy in bookshops, they're not by ordinary people. It's like teapots, you don't imagine that there's a pot maker who made a teapot. You know they're things you buy in a shop. Somehow bringing the creation of this into the land of real people, we need to do that early.

There's nothing magic about symbols, it's just that it's another way of having words. We have words by speech, by letters, by signs, by pictures – it's all part of the multi-media world we live in. We just need to see it as all part of that same thing. About communicating both on paper and verbally. The only thing about communicating on paper is that we've seen now a lot of evidence that the writing process helps with the logic of thinking and the structuring of ideas. By being able to write and put things down, retrieve them, mess with them, change them – it helps with your whole thinking processes, it does a lot more than just develop you literacy. Again, if you can't do that because you can't write text you're losing a whole lot of the learning process.

N.P. It ties up with something I was thinking about the other day: in a lot of work on mathematics, youngsters have actually to write down what they've been doing. I was interested that in watching someone do it the other day, exactly the process you were describing went on. I was thinking to myself, had it been someone who found it easier to use symbols, there's all sorts of things you could have done there.

I'd better ask you the question from the distrustful teacher, which is: Won't all these symbols stop my children learning to read or write? Do you know what I mean?

T.D. Yes I understand the question. The answer is that we don't know, but I've seen no evidence that it will do. There was always an argument and I know this is still contentious in some places, that if you teach somebody to sign (I'm talking about people with poor speech, rather than Deaf people) that they won't speak. What we have discovered is that actually if you teach people to communicate, they will want to communicate more. I think that writing in symbols is about the same thing. We talk about emergent literacy experiences turning pages, holding books – if we can turn pages and hold books, maybe we can also model the writing process.

There's a teacher in a school in Birmingham, Dave Wood, who gets his kids doing scribble writing. They have physical disabilities so they scribble write by pressing the concept keyboard. They just get any old symbols up in the same way as any child with a pencil would do lots of wiggles for scribble writing. What we can do is to bring those emergent and pre-literacy experiences to the same kids.

A colleague of mine teaches at an EBD school and he was showing those books I was talking about, the ones written by teenagers for other kids, to his EBD students and they said 'Oh we don't need those pictures'. He said 'Of course you don't need those pictures, but I just wanted you to look at them because these are written for little children'. 'Oh fine, we'll look at them' and of course what he found was that they were reading them more easily actually because the pictures were there. But because we are such a textbound society actually we'd look at the text first. If I show you a page of symbols and text you will read the text unless I remove it. You will only look at the pictures second. Also, the nice thing about technology is that you can change the proportions so you could have big symbols and little words or big words and little tiny symbols. You can just put symbols for the words that are likely to be difficult. You haven't got to have all symbols or all words – we could put a picture in just for the words that you're struggling with.

N.P. The National Literacy Strategy includes some Widgit symbols. Could you discuss the use of symbols in the way the National Literacy Strategy appears to be developing?

T.D. I'm slightly bemused by it. In the word level module, there is a great pack of teachers' resource materials, loads of ideas and activities, really great and loads of symbols in them. The symbols are simply there as flash cards really, so that you know we want to find the 'ch' words, so there's pictures of chairs and things to cue you in. That's quite good because it's making a link between meaning, between the meaning of a word and what it represents. Some children actually need that concrete representation.

What it totally fails to do is still make that bridge for those children who are not yet ready to make the association between the series of letters and an idea. So all this bit that we're talking about: literacy, learning, sequencing, communicating meaning, isn't there. It's all about spelling and grammar but it's not actually about communication and it's certainly nothing to do with creativity, that I could see.

It's a great pity because we actually just want a slight redefinition of literacy. If we define literacy as expressing and understanding meaning from print, we can then start to accommodate all sorts of children who use print but not necessarily single letters. They can go through all of this business of associating meaning, about expressing ideas, about understanding of the world; we can bring in this wonderful wealth of literature we have around us because we can support it with other things.

So, what's it about? Is it only about decoding text or is it about meanings and expression? Poetry is fascinating because it has wonderful rhythm and sound and the whole thing is a magic way of dealing with language. Every child learns through nursery rhymes and nonsense rhymes. Somehow, once you get to seven, that goes. Somehow, if you've got learning difficulties you don't get this stuff and why not? Absolutely, why not?

The horror is of seeing ten year olds still doing nursery rhymes when we've got wonderful things around that we could be using. What's quite interesting about that is when you do the Shakespeare *thing 'Is this a dagger I see before me?'* Do you use the symbol of the word before that conjures up the word *before* with a temporal meaning, or do you use the spatial one which actually interprets as *in front*. Correctly, a speech therapist might say; 'I would use the symbol for *in front* because that's what I mean but if you read 'Is this a dagger I see in front of me?', somehow it just doesn't have the same kind of zap about it. If it's a clue into the sound then we use the symbols to make the sounds, if it's a clue into an exact meaning, then you use the symbol for the meaning.

I don't see anything wrong in saying 'Well sometimes, we use one and sometimes, we use the other.' I think we've got too precious and it comes back to what I said before. Kids are actually quite resilient; they understand. If they're going to understand the difference anyway, they're going to understand about time and space and then that gives you another topic of conversation.

N.P. So in other words, what we're saying is that this is a way into literature as well as anything else.

T.D. I think we are in a multi-media society, we think and we expect, high quality images. All the time now the naff little hand-drawing on the wall somehow is just not it – we're in a different league. So I think exchanging information and exchanging what our kids do and what we do is very important. I think we have to make sure that we're getting the right media all the time and I think that just because we now have whizzy technology that allows us to put video on the Internet, it doesn't mean to say that we *have* to put video on the Internet. There's a really good thing about videoing a piece of drama or action that children do in order that you can look at and review it. So you can share video in the same way that writing is both a method of recording an idea and sharing it and becoming a publisher. I think that to become a film maker or a producer of drama is something within the bounds now of all children. That I think is an important experience. I don't think we necessarily have to confuse the communications technologies with that experience.

N.P. A final question: How do you see this system developing, particularly in terms of its international possibilities?

T.D. There is a project which we're part of which is looking at enabling people to e-mail in symbols. One of the problems that you have, if you have learning difficulty or a communication difficulty, is that you tend to communicate only with people who are close to you and who you are very familiar with. So you don't have the benefit of exploring ideas with newcomers and strangers, communicating with distance. So what we want to do is bring that experience into the realms of people with learning difficulties. Now we don't know what sense they will make of it, we don't know to what extent people will understand that I can talk about football with somebody who is in Portugal. But actually if we've got something in common, why don't we? One of the beautiful things about symbols, about graphics, is that a football is a football and it doesn't matter what kind of sound you attach to it, the concept of a football looks like this so I can actually talk to you even though you're a Portuguese speaker and I'm an English speaker.

What we're exploring at the moment in the project is, to what extent can we make this happen and not worry about the culture around this. We want to learn from the Deaf community so we don't have a different sign language in every single language. We are fortunate because there are very few pictorial languages and in fact we are working very closely with an American symbol company in order to merge the two sets. Hopefully we will end up with a single approach. I don't want to say that anybody's got to have a monopoly because you can't have a monopoly. These are words; there shouldn't be copyrights, they should be free (although actually somebody has to be paid for drawing them) but this is language. What if we could have a single graphic language that is used in any culture and just extend it?

They've been using this in Papua New Guinea where a school building is under a tree there, so they have a different picture of school from here. At least if I see school sent to me from Papua New Guinea I have a picture of what school means to them. I think it has huge international possibilities which we are only just glimpsing at the moment.

Chapter 10

Principles for use and evaluation

Steven Fawkes

Based on all of the foregoing reports this chapter summarises the educational rationale for using and making video in the classroom, and identifies criteria for evaluating resources. A schedule for use in a record system is included.

Viewing television on video presents opportunities for:

- social viewing;
- observing processes and methods of doing / making things;
- establishing a theme;
- introducing language or concepts;
- supporting and enhancing curriculum content;
- pausing to focus on relevant details and images;
- observing things which are distant and unfamiliar;
- exploring concepts of time;
- stimulating drama and creative work;
- developing media awareness:
    recognising special effects
    distinguishing fantasy scenes
    interpreting messages
    aesthetic judgements

Making video presents opportunities for:

- creating curriculum resources;
- recording an event;
- creating a narrative;
- recording achievement;
- boosting self-esteem;
- promoting a school;
- collating personal contributions;
- developing technical skills.

When viewing a television resource with a learning purpose in mind it is useful to keep the following questions foremost:

Evaluating resources

- Is the programme age-appropriate?
- Is the content relevant to the teaching and learning plan?
- Will pupils / students identify with the people in the programme?
- Are the presenters of the programme well enough known?
- Are the images clear and stimulating?
- Is the language level appropriate to the class?
- Can the concepts, sequences or discussion points be identified easily?
- Is it an enjoyable resource?

There may well be other criteria of importance to a particular class, and it is unlikely that every programme resource will score well in all of the categories identified, but continuing experimentation with television resources and strategies for their use will sharpen perceptions of what is or is not likely to be useful.

Teachers working in collaboration may like to use an evaluation form such as the one at the end of this chapter in order to compare views and experiences or to keep a record of useful programmes in the Resource Base.

Detailed Evaluation Schedule with commentary

General
Title of the programme / series:
Target age (if stated):
If a target age is not stated, what seems likely?
The information above is critical and the identified Target Group should be borne in mind when the relevance of the items below is checked.

Stimulus
Does it provide good clear images and sound?
Does it allow for easy interruption for explanation, repetition or questioning?
Does it provoke learners to wish to interrupt themselves to ask questions or add comments?

Motivation
A programme can present different sorts of motivational features (music, drama, animation, content, humour).
Will the overall design of this programme appeal to the target group of learners?
Is it an appropriate style or genre?
Does it provide a range of different speakers?
Are the people in the programme interesting?
Does it provide a variety of inputs that could be useful?
i.e. drama, song, verse, narrative.

Level
Does it fit with the maturity level of the teaching group?
Is the language level largely appropriate to the target group?
Does it include any in-built repetition?
This may be important for some teaching groups, and will have implications for how the programme is used with them.

Context
Do the visual elements help clarify the language appropriately through context clues?

Flexibility
Is the content of the programme relevant to the scheme of work and/or the learners' needs and interests?
Are the segments of the programme of the right length for this group?
Would sections of the programme interest other teaching groups?

Ease of use
Are there programme segments?

Other criteria
These may relate to general issues such as gender balance or the multicultural mix, or to particular issues such as the use of 'pieces to camera' which allow for close viewing of lip movements.

Chapter 11

Video journalism project

Maureen Smith

Maureen Smith of Mental Health Media outlines a partnership project in the field of developing video skills

Fastforward was a project run by Mental Health Media from May 1994–May 1996. It looked at ways in which people with learning difficulties could gain access to video. The project finished in June 1996.

Whatever happened to Fastforward?

The project includes:

The video journalism project

- A Video Journalism course for people with learning difficulties with accreditation from the Open College Network.
- The production of three video magazines about vocational training opportunities for people with learning difficulties in Europe (made by trainees on our Video Journalism courses).
- A website aimed at people with learning difficulties which gives information about the project and opportunity to share ideas about work, training and media.

The Video Journalism Project is part funded by the European Union's Leonardo de Vinci programme, Mencap and Mental Health Media. The project works across Holland, Ireland and the UK and uses the media to look at vocational training opportunities for people with learning difficulties in each of these member states. Partners in the project are: Mencap, Mental Health Media, People First of Europe (UK), Bilancia, Brothers of Charity, London Open College Network, National Institute of Continuing Adult Education, Focus Central London (Training and Enterprise Council).

A partnership approach

Video journalism course

Mental Health Media has responsibility for delivering the video journalism course. It ran its first pilot video journalism course in West London from September 1997–March 1998. There were seven trainees on the course who learnt about using camcorders, health and safety, research, interview and editing techniques. As part of the course, they travelled to visit groups in the UK, Holland and Ireland to film people in work skills training and employment. Everyone passed the course and all of them achieved three credits at level one which was the maximum award of credits available.

A second pilot course started in July 1998 in Northampton and is being run in conjunction with Northampton People First. In the first part of the course, guest speakers included two people who attended the first course in London and members of Bristol Self-Advocacy Research Group who shared their experience of conducting successful research projects. Involving people with learning difficulties as trainers is something we aim to build on in the future.

Other groups are running the course from January 1999. Course materials will be distributed over the Internet along with details of how to register with a local Open College Network centre. Details can also be sent in the post at cost of photocopying and postage.

Work in Europe (video magazine)

'Work in Europe' is the first of three video magazines which looks at training and employment opportunities for people with learning difficulties in Ireland, Holland and the UK. It was made by people with learning difficulties who attended the Video Journalism Course in 1997.

There are five items in the video:

- A mountain shop in North Wales where people with Learning Difficulties are trained to work as mechanics.
- A cleaning cooperative in Bristol, run by people with learning difficulties.
- A gardening enterprise in Holland.
- A charity in Ireland which organises work placements for people.
- A project in Chelmsford which offers training and employment opportunities.

Website

Our website can be found at: www.mediafirst.org.uk.

Chapter 12

The Future

Julie Cogill

As technological advances bring more flexibility and more equipment into the learning situation, Julie Cogill reflects on some of the advantages and disadvantages that may come with them.

Some time ago I judged a schools video competition and one of the prize winners was a special school. The film was made by a group of young people with learning difficulties aged twelve or thirteen and there was no doubt that it was their own work. The focus of the video was the local village and it was being made so that younger children in the school could appreciate the environment they live in. Local shopkeepers were interviewed and local viewers were presented. There were two shots however that particularly interested me: the first was a pan around the village green which crawled noticeably very slowly round all the features of the green; the second was a shot of the local war memorial which must have been held for seven or eight seconds, so long that it was clearly difficult to keep the camera from hovering up and down whilst taking the shot. What has always interested me about the film is:

- were the group doing the filming, instructed to make these shots very slowly and hold them for a long time by their teacher?
- was this the style they naturally adopted for themselves?
- was this the style that the group perceived would be best for the younger children in their school?

Unfortunately, I never managed to find the answers to these questions but what the story emphasises is the need to consider the rate at which people digest information and the pace at which we generally give information to people. This is particular true for children and young people with learning disabilities.

The future, we all hear, will provide huge potential for learning through technology, but will it?

In 3000 BC the speed of transmission of information depended on a runner taking messages from place to place. The rate of transfer was about 0.01 words per minute assuming he or she was fit and didn't have to run too far. Gradually, horses began to be used to carry the messengers, thus increasing the speed until telegraph was invented which took transmission up to 60 words per minute.

Today, via fibre optic cables the speed of transmission is 100,000,000,000 or one hundred billion words per minute. However, let's think for a moment about human information processing. In 3000 BC the human mind could absorb information at the rate of 300 words per minute and what is it today? Not surprisingly, still 300 words per minute! Some things have changed but others remain the same. We cannot expect the increasing speed of digital processing to accelerate the processes of learning in direct proportion.

So where does the future take us to? Television and video already provides wonderful access to children with learning difficulties. Many of the experiences described in this book transport children to worlds they would never otherwise experience.

The wider world

TV allows access to view natural phenomena: animals in their natural habitat, earthquakes and volcanoes. Children can visit distant and inaccessible places, and hear viewpoints from people in different parts of the world.

The historical world

Film of historical sites, archive material and dramatisations provide sources of evidence and insight into past events.

The micro and macro world

Video material helps with the understanding of physical and scientific processes through film of dangerous experiments, slow motion and time lapse photography to demonstrate dynamic change over very short or very long periods of time; magnification through an electron microscope brings to life outer space, microscopic particles and even the inside of the human body.

The emotional world

TV and radio give access to the views and experiences of others through case study material and drama reconstructions to enable empathy with others' situations, and to stimulate personal views on difficult issues or events.

The conceptual world

Through graphic sequences, animation and the instantaneous move from concrete to abstract, TV enables children to consolidate their understanding of concepts in many different ways.

Relevance

The Four Rs

Schools programmes are specifically designed for each age group to ensure that learning outcomes are always relevant to the National Curriculum. Programmes produced for children with learning disabilities are made to take account of the need for more repetition, longer shots and more careful explanation.

Reliability

Programmes are carefully researched to provide the most up-to-date and reliable source of information.

Remembering

Film resources help children to remember information more easily through interesting case studies, use of cartoons, humour and drama to create motivation and interest in the material to be learned. A lot of information can be transferred very quickly through TV and pictures can sometimes explain a thousand words.

Range

Programmes are accessible across a wide range of abilities. They are an invaluable resource for children with learning difficulties particularly if access to learning via books isnot an option.

However video, as we know it, is no longer the only visual medium available. The idea that TV will converge with ICT over the next few years (time span currently unpredictable) is not new. But what are the advantages of these new learning systems?

Whether delivered by CD ROM, the Internet, standard computer software or digital television the key lies in the potential for interactivity. An interactive system allows learners to direct their own pace, to view a section several times, to jump forward or backwards in a programme, or to access further information if their understanding is not clear. It gives feedback and can encourage people to respond at certain points and provides the facility to retread the learning path if necessary.

The interactive multi-media resource of the future will provide the possibility for the learner to:

- have one-to-one attention;
- input his/her own views and ideas;
- direct the pace of learning;
- gain feedback on understanding during the process of learning;
- have access to information in many varied forms;
- access a motivating, exciting and individual experience;
- interact with other learners across the globe;
- create his/her own multi-media note book for future use.

For children with learning disabilities the most important factors in 'viewing' multimedia resources must be the facility to control what they are seeing, to direct their own pace, to revisit learning points easily and have access to information in many varied forms. In terms of 'making' their own resources learners will be able to use what they have found to compose their own creations, assembling moving images with photographs, sound, symbols or text flexibly.

All of these features enhance the potential for developing independence, by giving increasingly more control to the learners of the resources they are using. Clearly, in practical terms, some students (and teachers) will have more facility with new technology than others, but this source of control promises to give a high boost to confidence.

The potential for learning activity through digital means in the future is tremendous. I believe, however, there is still a great deal of work to be done on managing multi-media interactive resources and creating the style of software that is most appropriate for maximum learning potential for learners of a wide range of ability. With clarity of vision the use of new technologies for children and young people with learning difficulties will hugely enhance their Access to Learning in the next century.

Useful organisations

SENJIT – Special Educational Needs – Joint Initiative for Training, University of London Institute of Education, 20, Bedford Way, London, WC1H 0AL Tel. 0171 612 6273
Internet: http://www.ioe.ac.uk/teepnnp/SENJIT_Home.html

BBC Education, White City, 201, Wood Lane, London W12 7TS
Information: Tel. 0181 746 1111
Internet: http://www.bbc.co.uk/education

NCET – National Council for Educational Technology is now called BECTa

BECTa – British Educational Communications and Technology agency, Milburn Hill Road, Science Park, Coventry CV4 7JJ
Tel. 01203 416 994
Internet: http://www.becta.org.uk

Suggested reading

Approaches to teaching pupils with severe learning difficulties

Carpenter, B., Ashdown, R. and Bovair, K. (eds) (1996) *Enabling Access*. London: David Fulton.

Coupe, J. and Goldbart, J. (1998) *Communication Before Speech: Development and Assessment*. London: David Fulton.

Dunn, J. (1991) 'Understanding others: evidence from naturalistic studies of children.' Whiten, A. (ed.) *Natural Theories of Mind*. Oxford, Blackwell.

Harris, J. (1988) *Language Development in schools for children with Severe Learning Difficulties*. London: Croom Helm.

Lewis, V., Boucher, J. and Astell, A. (1992) 'The assessment of symbolic play in young children: a prototype test'. *European Journal of Disorders of Communication*, **27**, 231–245.

NCC (1992a) *NCC Curriculum Guidance 9. The National Curriculum for pupils with Severe Learning Difficulties*.

NCC (1992b) *NCC Curriculum Guidance 10. Teaching Science to pupils with Special Educational Needs*.

Piaget, J. and Inhelder, B. (1956) *The Child's Conception of Space*. London: Routledge and Kegan Paul.

Smith, B. (ed.) *The National Curriculum for pupils with Severe Learning Difficulties: Interactive approaches to teaching core subjects*. Bristol: Lame Duck Publications.

Sensory impairment issues

Beverley Schools Communication Link. Available from Beverley Schools for the Deaf, Beverley Road, Saltersgill, Middlesborough, Cleveland TS4.

Dictionary of British Sign Language. Produced by the British Deaf Association, and available from booksellers.

My Turn to Speak. A useful resource package on using communication aids is available from the Wolfson Centre, Mecklenburgh Square, London WC1N 2AP. Price £75.00

Signalong Phase 1, Phase 2 & PSE. Available from Mike Kennard, 129 Rochester Road, Burham, Rochester ME1 3SG.

Sign and Say Books 1 & 2. Available from RNID, 105 Gower Street, London WC1.

Smith, Cath (1990) *Signs Make Sense*. London: Souvenir Press.

Carver, G. (1994) 'A Survey of Teachers' "Perceptions" of the Effects on Children of the New Entertainment Technologies', *The SLD Experience*. Issue 9. Summer.

Choat, E. and Griffin, H. (1989) *Using Television in the Primary School*. RKP.

Cogill, J. (1993) 'Television and Learning', *The SLD Experience*. Issue 5. Spring.

Grove, N. (1998) *Literature for All*. London: David Fulton.

Hunt, A. (1995) 'The Power of the Screen-written Word', *Child Education*, February.

Hutchins, J. (1995) 'IT and Dyslexia', *Interactive Magazine*. Issue 1. July.

McKeown, S. and Thomas, M. 'Helping children with Special Educational Needs', in McKeown, S. and Thomas, M. *A Parents' Guide to Computers*.

Mumford, S. *The Really Useful Media Book*. Wakefield TVEI.

NCET. *Operating Up The Library for Visually Impaired Learners*.

Nimmo, C. (1994) 'Autism and Computers', *Communication: The Journal of the National Autistic Society*. **28**, Issue 2. Summer.

Zihni, F. and F. (1995) 'The AZ Method in communication', *The Journal of the National Autistic Society*, Summer.

Teaching children with learning difficulties using television and multimedia

Video resource

Lilly and Cogo (Jaritz, Hyvarinen and Schaden).
This Swedish programme was designed especially for children with low vision. It has short, slow-moving stories involving children with familiar objects, and associated dolls and picture books which help pupils to attach meaning to what they see on the screen. Details from Olga Millar, RNIB Education Centre, Garrow House, 190 Kensal Road, London W10.

Dominguez, B. and Dominguez, J. (1991) *Building Blocks*. New York: American Foundation for the Blind.

Gregory, R.L. (1990) *Eye and Brain: The Psychology of Seeing*. London: Weidenfeld and Nicolson.

Harrell, L. and Akeson, N.(1987). *Preschool vision stimulation: Itís more than a flashlight!* New York: American Foundation for the Blind.

Hello! Visual stimulation video for use in the classroom or for parents to use at home. Available from RNIB Booksales, 190 Kensal Road, London W10, 5BT.

Pogrund, L., Fazzi, D.L. and Lampert, S. (eds) (1992) *Early Focus: Working with Blind and Visually Impaired Children and Their Families*. New York: American Foundation for the Blind.

The RNIB Service for Children and Young People with Multiple Disabilities can provide further information and help in relation to Cortical Visual Impairment.

Visual Stimulation

Bruner, J. S. (1986) *Actual Minds, Possible Worlds*. Cambridge, Mass. Harvard University Press.

Cazden, C.B. (1983) 'Play with language and metalinguistic awareness: one dimension of language experience', Donaldson, M., Grieve, R. and Pratt, C. (eds) *Early Childhood Development and Education*. Oxford: Blackwell.

Department for Education (1995) *English in the National Curriculum*. London: HMSO.

Dunn, J. (1991) 'Understanding others: evidence from naturalistic studies of children', Whiten, A. (ed.) *Natural Theories of Mind*. Oxford: Blackwell.

It all comes out in the wash: Using TV 'soaps' with pupils with learning disabilities

Flavell, J., Speer, J. and Green, F.L. (1983) 'Development of the appearance-reality distinction', *Cognitive Psychology*, **15**, 95–120.

Heathcote, D (1980) *Drama as Context*. Huddersfield: NATE.

Hinchcliffe, V. (1995a) The social cognitive development of children with severe learning difficulties. Unpublished PhD thesis, Brunel University.

Hinchcliffe, V. (1995b) 'English' in Carpenter, B.R. Ashdown and K. Bovair (eds) *Enabling Access*. London: David Fulton.

Hinchcliffe, V. and Roberts, M. (1987) 'Developing social cognition and metacognition', in Smith, B. (ed.) *Interactive Approaches to the Education of Children with Severe Learning Difficulties*, Westhill College.

Hobson, R.P. (1993) *Autism and the Development of Mind*. Hove: LEA.

Lloyd, B. and Goodwin, R. (1995) 'Let's pretend: casting the characters and setting the scene' *British Journal of Developmental Psychology*, **13**, 261–270.

Nelson, K. (1981) 'Social cognition in a script framework', in Flavell, J.H. and Ross L. (eds) *Social Cognitive Development*. Cambridge: Cambridge University Press.

Premack, D. and Woodruff, G. (1978) 'Does the chimpanzee have a theory of mind?' *Behavioral and Brain Sciences*, **1**, 515–26.

Staff of Rectory Paddock School (1983) *In Search of a Curriculum*, Robin Wren Publications.

BBC Access to Learning

The *Access to Learning* project at the BBC embraces television programmes and accompanying resources to support particular groups of learners in need of specific support. At the time of writing the *Access to Learning* initiative has commissioned television programmes under three headings:

Learners with Severe Learning Difficulties
Profoundly Deaf children
Children for whom English is an Additional Language.

The programmes relevant to children and older students with Severe Learning Disabilities are entitled:

Go for it!
Go for it! Choices
Go for it! Lifeskills

As indicated by the initial research with schools these programmes aim to offer access to areas of the curriculum at the same time as offering positive role-models, and peer group representation.

Publications supporting these series have enjoyed collaboration with colleagues at *Widget Software*, in order to integrate symbols into the worksheets for students needing them.

Three special programmes have also been made in the *Documentary Scrapbook* strand. These offer versions of documentaries compiled from mainstream educational broadcasts and re-edited to provide more discussion time, and less busy presentations, for teachers and learners to work with.

Information about transmissions of these programmes may be obtained from BBC Education Information, BBC White City, 201, Wood Lane, London W12 7TS.

Index